T0286110

NINE
FIGURE
MINDSET

HOW TO GO FROM ZERO TO
OVER $100 MILLION
IN NET WORTH

BRANDON DAWSON

I want to dedicate my book to my amazing three daughters: Samantha, Brianna, and Ciara, and to my father and mother.

I also want to dedicate this book to all of my most impactful mentors: Jim Dawson, Bill Austin, John C. Maxwell, Jim Collin's, Hector LaMarque, Robert Anthony, Sharon Lechter, Story Musgrave, Doug Good, Marc Still, Baron Cass, John Strauss, and Grant and Elena Cardone.

But most importantly, I dedicate my life to my remarkable wife and business partner Natalie Dawson.
Thank you all for inspiring me, teaching me, loving me, and being patient with me while I grow and learn.

Nine-Figure Mindset: How to Go from Zero to Over $100 Million in Net Worth
Copyright © 2023 by Brandon Dawson

All rights reserved. No part of this publication may be reproduced, stored in a retrieval system, or transmitted in any form by any means, electronic, mechanical, photocopy, recording, or otherwise, without the prior permission of the publisher, except as provided by USA copyright law.

No patent liability is assumed with respect to the use of the information contained herein. Although every precaution has been taken in the preparation of this book, the publisher and author assume no responsibility for errors or omissions. Neither is any liability assumed for damages resulting from the use of the information contained herein.

Published by Maxwell Leadership Publishing, an imprint of Forefront Books. Distributed by Simon & Schuster.

Library of Congress Control Number: 2023910825

Print ISBN: 979-8-88710-026-5
E-book ISBN: 979-8-88710-027-2

Cover Design by George Stevens, G Sharp Design LLC
Interior Design by PerfecType, Nashville, TN

CONTENTS

FOREWORD

John C. Maxwell

Brandon Dawson always credits me with being a force that changed his life, but I think it's just as true to say that he changed mine.

Let me explain.

During the period from 2000–2002 when Brandon was creating the blueprint for what would become his second company, Audigy, he read several of my books as carefully as anybody ever has. After he launched Audigy in 2004, he continued to use my books, along with many others, and his company became the most dominant player in the hearing health industry in America. By then, I had followed Brandon's success with admiration, and I appreciated his kind words to me about the impact my teachings had made in his development as a leader.

Anyone who has written a book knows what I mean!

We finally met in person in 2012 when Brandon invited me to come to Las Vegas and speak at an Audigy meeting. Nothing in our previous correspondence prepared me for what I saw in Las Vegas. Sometimes you meet someone and feel like you've known them your whole life. That's the way I felt when I first met Brandon. Still, I was surprised by the skill with which my "old friend" led the hundreds of business owners who were gathered there.

It was like being in church. Brandon was magnetic! I marveled—and felt humbled—when I heard some of the ideas that I'd written about over the years being incorporated, expanded, and *improved upon* by Brandon right there on the stage.

Brandon was not only teaching his team the principles in my books, he was also showing them how to apply them and create a game plan they could easily follow. I do a lot of leadership coaching and training for organizations around the world, including governments, as well as businesses of all sizes and levels of complexity. Some are in rough shape and suffer from weak leadership before my company, Maxwell Leadership, arrives on the scene. Others are further along the leadership spectrum and work with us to make themselves better.

Brandon's team fell into neither camp, exactly, because Brandon gets it like nobody I've ever met. And by "it," I mean how to create systems that foster leadership up and down organizational culture in a way people can understand. My role at the meeting was to help Brandon deepen and enrich his team's thinking. I was happy to do so.

I thought so highly of what I saw there that, in 2013, I invited Brandon to come work with my team at Maxwell Leadership. Following the methodology Brandon developed at Audigy, we broke everyone into teams—including operations, marketing, finance, and so on—and applied Brandon's techniques to optimize our systems and processes, while aligning each team member's goals with those of our organization. A decade later, we continue to apply Brandon's best practices, which have helped us grow and prosper as an organization and as individuals.

I had never thought of myself as a writer until I had a conversation with the author of several great books who told me he wrote not because he needed to write but to extend his influence beyond his personal touch. This single conversation led to a writing career with more than one hundred books to my credit. And by the way, I'm still writing and loving every minute of it.

Each time you finish writing a book, you feel relieved but also a little bit anxious because you hope that what you've worked so hard to share with others will actually change the way they work and live. You don't change lives by writing a book; you change lives when readers act on what they learn.

This is why I am so delighted that Brandon has chosen to write *Nine-Figure Mindset: How to Go from Zero to Over $100 Million in Net Worth* at this moment in his remarkable career. Although his boundless energy and passion for helping small business owners to prosper has enabled him to touch thousands of lives personally through his management companies—most recently, Cardone Ventures, which he co-founded with Grant Cardone—I am confident this book will enable Brandon to reach millions more who have a dream of succeeding as a small business owner and leader.

Why am I so confident? Because there is nobody out there today who can connect the dots between leading and succeeding quite the way Brandon does in page after page of this, what I hope will be only his *first* book.

This book is for leaders who manage a few people, who manage many people, and even who manage only themselves at the present time. This book is for the founder still struggling internally to justify hiring that first employee even though he or she has grown frustrated by having to do everything themselves. It is for the business leader who may have hired a handful of employees only to discover that they don't share the same passion for the business he or she does. But mostly it's for the business leader who knows the business and industry cold but never learned how to lead others because, truth be told, leading others well is hard to do.

Organizations rarely, if ever, suffer from a lack of *followership*. What's usually found wanting is leadership. And the most important part of leadership that goes missing is neither intelligence nor technical know-how; it's the business owner's ability to align the organization's success with that of each team member's vision of success.

Creating this kind of alignment takes a leader who understands, and has the integrity to act on, the knowledge that leadership is about creating value for other people, not just the business owner. It is about showing people you really do care so they, in turn, do everything in their power to contribute to your shared success.

Before we can hope to lead others, however, we must learn how to lead ourselves, which means learning all there is to know about our own hopes, fears, dreams, and goals. After all, if we don't know what motivates and inspires us, how can we hope to motivate and inspire others?

The crowning achievement of Brandon's book, *Nine-Figure Mindset: How to Go from Zero to Over $100 Million in Net Worth*, is to connect the dots between the practice of leading oneself and leading others to expect more out of our businesses, careers, and lives. Make no mistake: those dots *have to be connected*. There is no easy way forward, no "hack" that lets you bypass the doubts, setbacks, crises, and even failures that attend any adventure worth taking. But if you follow Brandon's advice and, more importantly, his well-told example of devoting your career to creating value for others, you will discover, as I have, that your life is immeasurably better.

And in my book, better is always the goal.

It's Okay to Dream and to Dream BIG!

I wrote this book for *you*, the dreamers who fully under-stand that you have the power to create the life you want, no matter what your circumstances. The ones who are dreaming big and going against the status quo, who are willing to fail in order to make your dreams come true. The ones who never ever settle. Let me, a high school graduate with a 2.4 GPA, who sat on a tractor in his parents' walnut orchard and dreamed of owning his own business one day, be a living testament to you, wherever you find yourself in your entrepreneurial journey.

I've started, scaled, and grown multiple companies, creating financial abundance for myself and everyone else in my organizations. Just to give one example, in 2004 I created Audigy Group, a management company that provided 360-degree consulting and operational services to small businesses in the hearing services industry. In 2016, I went on to sell the company—a company I self-funded—for an astonishing $151 million, seventy-seven times EBITDA (earnings before interest, taxes, depreciation, and amortization). It was one of the highest values ever paid for a private company. One of the best days of my life was the day I sent out $35 million to my teams and customers who had been part of helping me grow and scale the business. After we sold the business using the same strategies and methodologies we used to grow our business, we were able to grow a $1 billion business to $4.5 billion in thirty-six months.

Then I turned my attention to working with a legendary sales genius to co-create a multi-billion-dollar company that serves small business owners just like you. Through several lifetimes' worth of experiences, partners, customers, mentors, employees, trusted advisors, and business acquisitions, along with the ability to learn how to embrace the struggle and completely shift my mindset, I was then, and only then, able to change the entire trajectory of my life.

I want to help *you* change or accelerate yours. In the pages that follow, I'm going to give you no-nonsense business practices and advice that you can implement and execute today to help you not only transform your business, but all areas of your life. You'll read real and raw stories about my journey (the highs and the lows), plus the journeys of other business owners just like you who I've partnered with or helped in recent years, to illustrate how these key principles work when applied. As you will see, many have transformed their businesses.

I want you to skip all the mistakes I made so you can learn to leverage both the successes and failures of *your* journey. It is my belief that from our greatest failures comes the potential for incredible opportunity through stepping back for a moment, allowing ourselves the luxury—no, the necessity—of rewiring our brains, and learning how to move forward, creating success with great intentionality.

▪ ▪ ▪

The first thing you need to know is that success isn't easy. There are 31.5 million small to midsize businesses in the United States. According to national statistics, 97 percent of new companies will fail within their first ten years. Being a small business owner who's built a career working with other small business owners, I have made it my personal passion to prevent perfectly good businesses—businesses that provide great products and services to customers—from failing simply because the owners don't know how business growth works.

This raises some questions: Why do some businesses succeed while others fail? What do successful business owners know that others don't know? I think there are several answers to these questions, and all are addressed in this book. But for the moment, let's look at the underlying dynamic that takes place in the hearts and minds of the business owners I have known (and I've known thousands of them). Understanding these dynamics, even superficially at first, will prepare you to read this book with greater focus and insight.

First is the question of whom you listen to. I have dear friends and I have dear mentors. On rare occasions, a close mentor becomes a close friend. But the two relationships are not the same thing. A friend loves us for who we are, warts and all. A mentor sees who we can become and helps us get there. A mentor may or may not love you, though they will probably at least like you. The biggest mistake you can make is to listen to friends, family members, loved ones, professors, business brokers, lawyers, accountants, and all the people who want to offer you advice but haven't actually done what you are trying to do. The fastest way to succeed is to find the closest example of what you want to accomplish and model yourself after the person who achieved it.

So, who is a mentor? A mentor is someone who has what you want, who is the kind of person you'd like to be, and who has done the kind of thing you want to do. That last part of the sentence should be your guide: listen to people who have done what you want to do. The reason I am calling this book a business biography is that I have done what you want to do. The purpose of the book is to show how my life as an entrepreneur unfolded, including the mistakes I made and the lessons I learned. There will be chapters devoted to specific lessons and plenty of examples of other entrepreneurs and thought leaders who have either transformed my life or I theirs. But I feel as though I've led the kind of life that has the potential to be instructive to others who want to be successful business owners and leaders.

Born to humble working parents who divorced when I was young, I found myself spending more time with my mom and the man who became my stepdad. He was a true entrepreneur and was trying to build Starkey, a manufacturer of hearing aids. Suddenly, during my long stays with them at a relatively young age, I was thrust into the chaotic and often downright crazy life of a start-up with world-class ambition. I joined the family business, only to leave it later and strike out on my own—a young man who was equally confident and frightened out in the world. The hardships I overcame and the lessons I learned from my extended family (and the family I started as well) formed the backdrop against which I became who I am today.

That person is someone who has felt the pain of not knowing where to turn, turning anyway, living with the consequences of my decisions, and learning how to avoid making the same mistakes again. Along the way, I had the great fortune to realize that the biggest hurdles to my happiness in life were the things I didn't know I didn't know. I had the presence of mind, or maybe just the desperation, to apprentice myself to some extraordinary mentors who helped me reprogram my brain to replace fear and judgment with confidence and honesty.

Now I feel it is my duty to pass along my learning to you, the present and future generation of brave founders, entrepreneurs, business owners, and leaders.

Is there anything in that brief outline of my career that doesn't sound like something you'd like to achieve? Minus some of the mistakes, of course! Well, that's why I wrote this book: so you don't have to make the same mistakes I and so many others have made and continue to make.

Second is the question of how big you are thinking. Something I learned from one of my greatest mentors—and now friend and business partner in Cardone Ventures, Grant Cardone—is that most of us sell ourselves woefully short. Even those of us who think pretty highly of ourselves fall victim to underselling how far we can go. I have done years of homework and spent millions assessing the opportunities that would enable me to create unbelievable value by collaborating with entrepreneurs to change how small businesses are run. I built Audigy with the intention of proving that if, without using anybody else's money, I could figure out how to help business owners in the audiology space create massive value, I could do the same thing for hundreds of industries. This is what guided my hiring of research consultants to look at thousands of industries and to analyze test cases of reverse consolidation, the model for Audigy you'll read about in a later chapter.

After I sold Audigy for one of the highest values ever paid for a business, I had to stay on for three more years as part of the purchase price. I put my head down and, thirty-six months later and with an amazing team of leaders, we had turned a billion-dollar company into a four-billion-dollar company.

And then I was done. I found myself playing golf all the time and getting fat from too much going out to dinner. I'd earned everything I wanted in life, but I suddenly felt miserable because at the exact moment when I discovered my passion and zone of genius, I had no way to express it. I also felt fear—fear of losing what I had earned. Fear is a powerful demotivator for many business owners, and it was for me. Did I really have the courage to take this single-industry model I had perfected to hundreds of other industries? How would I do it?

My friend and mentor John Maxwell taught me the profound truth that making other people successful was the leader's responsibility. Later, when my wife, Natalie, introduced me to Grant's *The 10X Rule: The Only Difference between Success and Failure*, I knew I had to take renewed action and put my talents to use helping an even larger number of other people. When I first met Grant Cardone a few years ago, he said something to me that is now part of every thought, interaction, and action I take in my life: "Whatever you're thinking, Brandon . . . 10X that!" Grant also taught me that "success is your duty, obligation, and responsibility." I have thought about John's and Grant's words every day since, and I've made it a major theme of this book to reflect my determination, commitment, and duty to maximize my ability to the greater service of helping others take action in the pursuit of their dreams and goals as much as I possibly can.

At the core, the 10X concept exists to remind us all that we should always be thinking bigger and increasing our activity 10X more than we currently are. But in order to feel like we're worthy of those 10X dreams, we must first believe we are worthy of receiving them. And this introduces the next big question.

Third is the question of what kind of mindset successful business owners need to cultivate as though their lives depended on it, which to a large degree they do. You can have all the technical expertise in the world and the energy to match it, but unless you have a mindset that has been freed of self-limiting and self-sabotaging thoughts and feelings, and unless you can teach and coach your employees to be free of these as well, you will never achieve your goals and dreams. That may sound harsh, but it's the truth.

One of my most significant mentors, Story Musgrave, reinforced the power of belief through his own personal story. When I look at the totality of his career, from dropping out of high school, to being the only person to fly aboard all five space shuttles, he influenced me to think bigger, do more and have more courage. Story was instrumental in guiding me on how to build our operational platform to serve small business owners by connecting a "Mission Control" to help guide and assist them in their pursuit of excellence and value creation in the delivery of their products and services.

Perhaps the biggest struggle I've witnessed in thousands of employees and business owners over the years is the ability to move through self-limiting beliefs to find the resilience and tools that allow them to create the money and life and business they desire. Everything begins with mindset. Take a moment to ask yourself this: Are you living in a rich mindset or a poor mindset? If you want to grow personally, professionally, and financially, you have to align with people and ways of thinking and believing that support a rich mindset.

But before you can attract the kind of people to your project who can help you, you must take 100 percent of the accountability for your success. Only by looking into your own heart and mind and being clear on who you are and what your goals are can you build an organization of like-minded contributors.

Fourth is the question of who you bring along with you on your journey of success. Man, nothing is less productive and self-defeating than thinking you can do it all. It's a cliché that great entrepreneurs are not stubborn individualists but savvy collaborators who understand what they're good at and what they need help with; but you'd be amazed how many entrepreneurs still mess up when it comes to collaboration. In this book, you will learn how to collaborate by building a business in which everyone wins. You'll learn how to leverage the talents and goals of others—both your customers and your employees—so that everyone is working toward the same goal and vision based on the same values and mission.

The reason I called this book *Nine-Figure Mindset* is because I know that your success starts between your ears, and, as I started thinking about the millions of small business owners out there and recalling that 97 percent of them fail within ten years, I realized I wasn't executing my duty on the golf course. I recognized my duty was to help as many of those millions of small business owners as I possibly could to adjust their mindset and succeed rather than fail. Success is the legacy you will leave to all who cross your path, all whose lives you have improved along the way. All of us want to leave a legacy for future generations. A legacy not only paints a clear picture of the future you hope to see, but also establishes your priorities in the present.

As a scaling and turnaround expert who has a passion for helping business owners and their teams amplify their vision and impact through belief, strategy, execution, and leadership by building team alignment, I'm compelled now more than ever to share wisdom, insights, and perspectives to help others build their confidence through results. My mission is to teach you how to fight for your vision and purpose and set yourself (and everyone else around you) up to change your mind, change your life, and learn how to achieve your personal, professional, and financial goals.

That will be my legacy to entrepreneurs, and it is a legacy I am already putting in place through my work. In this book, you'll have the opportunity to hear from some of the small business owners I've worked with to help them transform their companies and their lives by implementing the principles discussed in this book.

■ ■ ■

This book is not only for you, the founder, entrepreneur, business owner, and leader, but also for your families and your teams. They are the ones who will go on the journey with you through the best of times and the worst of times. I guarantee you with 100 percent certainty that you are going to experience personal, professional, and possibly financial fear, anxiety, stress, frustration, and even possible failure in the growth process.

It is my intention to inspire you to fight your way through. That's going to be hard on you, but it's also going to take a big toll on your family and team. I can absolutely guarantee this.

But I can also guarantee with confidence that if you get to the other side of the struggle, your life and the lives of the people around you will be changed forever. You will have the ability and mindset to lead not only yourself but also others through every challenge—through whatever abyss stands between where you are now and your true potential for impact and success. Know that if you give up, those around you will also give up, and that if you develop true resilience and resourcefulness, those around you will discover the same qualities in themselves. Like attracts like. Birds of a feather flock together. They are clichés, but all clichés have an element of truth in them.

I want to open this book with the same challenge to you that I will close the book with. Ask yourself: Do I have the resilience and dedication to meet the obligation of success and be an example to others? Am I willing to challenge myself at all costs to follow my dream through whatever craziness it throws my way? I hope the answer is yes and that you will come to see that maybe you have undersold yourself *to yourself* regarding your capabilities. Whether or not you already own a business, I hope you will realize that the inkling you've felt that you should want more—and want to be more—is the reason you opened this book in the first place.

How do I know this? Because, dear reader, I was once in exactly the same place you are.

Let's dig in.

PART I

The Making of an Entrepreneur

CHAPTER 1

Tough Love from a Friend

"Pull over."

The order came from Hector LaMarque, my golfing buddy and friend, the guy who was sitting in the cart with me as we approached the ninth hole of the Bighorn Golf Club in Palm Desert. It was a beautiful Southern California day, but I hadn't really noticed the lush greenery or warming sunlight. I had spent the first eight holes bitching to Hector about all the bastards I'd had to deal with at my previous company.

Come to think of it, I'd been whining about them for a lot longer than eight holes—probably more on the order of twelve months. That's how long it had been since I'd been removed from my own company, the one I founded and grew by the sweat of my brow.

Hector wrote something down on his scorecard. I didn't love the way he looked at me as he handed it to me. On the scorecard was a simple phrase: "What you think is what you say. What you say is what you do. What you do is what you're known for. It's your legacy."

Then he looked me in the eye and said, "If you want to know where you're going in the future, just listen to what you're talking about right now. And what you're talking about now is everything that went wrong in the past." He continued, his eyes steadily holding mine, "So you're only going to find more of what you're focused on . . . things going wrong. And until you find what worked in the past and what you would do differently in the future, and accept responsibility for what you screwed up, you have no choice but to continue to fail forward.

"You are an amazingly talented person, but if that is what you are going to choose—to learn nothing and be the same—I refuse to be with you as your friend because you, Brandon, are better than that."

Ouch! I didn't see that one coming.

But that was the whole point, wasn't it? At the time, I was living way too much inside my own head and, as a result, was alienating one of the coolest people I knew. A guy who I viewed as my close friend was issuing a wake-up call. What was the matter with me?

I met Hector in 1999 and we quickly established a rapport. We shared a passion for golf and business and became golfing buddies. Hector is a good and honest man, fiercely loyal to his family and equally committed to his business. To my amazement, his most respected internal strengths—his confidence, charisma, and ability to connect with others—were reflected in the externals of his life as well. My first impression after meeting Hector was that he truly embodied the whole package: he was good-looking, charming, soft-spoken, and extremely respectful to people. His wife was amazingly beautiful and smart, and his children were extremely well-mannered. He had beautiful homes and traveled the world.

And he did all this while making millions of dollars each year as the founder of Performance Consulting Group, a Primerica Financial Services group that worked to build teams in the financial services sector. I thought of him as "Hector LaMarkable," and he was definitely someone I wanted to emulate in every way.

I couldn't have articulated it at the time, but my golfing buddy furnished all the living proof I needed to be reminded that when you're a good person on the inside, your life will mirror your mindset. I sensed that he had his priorities and values lined up just as true as a straight shot off the tee that lands with a gentle bounce, smack in the center of the fairway.

And now this guy for whom I had so much respect was telling me to stop being a drainer and stop acting like a victim all the time?

If you had seen the two of us buzzing around Bighorn Golf Club between 1999 and 2003, you would never have attached the word "victim" to either of us. We were among the exclusive club's youngest members and we both boasted five handicaps. We comfortably rubbed shoulders with millionaires and even the odd billionaire or two among those with whom we'd sit around after our golf rounds for drinks and a meal while we talked about business with the confidence that comes from knowing we'd built our companies from scratch.

Sometimes I would go to one of Hector's events as a guest to watch what he was doing. His world was very different from mine. I ran a corporation; he worked as a consulting service providing sales and development training for his teams in the financial services space. Hector and his people could absolutely pack a room with two thousand audience participants who all had given up their Saturdays for a dose of his mojo. I would sit and shake my head as his participants easily slipped into role-playing exercises and did the kind of stuff I couldn't even get my own employees to do.

"I'm on a mission to create million-dollar producers," Hector once told me. That gave me the idea to create million-dollar producers in the hearing space, which was my industry. But more on that later.

Our relationship was growing during a period that coincided with the terrorist attacks of September 11, 2001, when it felt like everyone we knew lost someone in the Towers. During this period, which devastated the American people and economy, his businesses continued to grow—Hector's just got bigger and bigger—and he continued to blow right through the tech industry crash that added to the economic misery.

My company was called Sonus Hearing Centers, which comprised a network of audiology clinics that sold hearing aids in the US and Canada. I started the company in January of 1996 after quitting the hearing aid manufacturing company created by my then stepdad, which had grown significantly with the help of my mom. That company, Starkey, grew from the humblest of beginnings to an organization valued at $350 million when I left it in December of 1995. It was a family-owned business and one I had worked at, on and off, since I was in the sixth grade. By the time I went to work there as an adult, it was a very serious player in its industry.

We'll get into the nitty-gritty of Starkey a bit later, but suffice it to say my experiences there taught me a few important things. First, it taught me most everything I needed to know about the hearing industry, which allowed me to make my own success in it after I left. And second, it taught me everything I needed to know about how to wear multiple hats, how to be resilient, and how to sell. But one of the things I did not learn was how to be a great leader—beginning with my own motivation for becoming an entrepreneur in the first place and including my total lack of leadership as a founder.

I thought I had quit Starkey because I didn't like the way the company was run, the constant infighting and power struggles practiced by its leadership team, and what I perceived as a lax leadership style that allowed too much room for underperformance. But the truth was that my wanting so badly to be successful played a big part in the company becoming such a jungle. Sure, I worked my way up the ladder and made some money for the company and myself with some clever ideas. But my ideas and successes usually came at someone else's expense, because my basic modus operandi was, "Hey, it's me against the world!"

People used to tell me I was walking on people. My retort was that you can't walk on people unless they are lying down.

When I started Sonus, I applied the same ego-driven approach to leadership—or what I understood to be leadership, which was me calling all the shots—that I'd seen in operation at Starkey. My business model was to buy up mostly small mom-and-pop audiology clinics whose owners were at, or nearing, retirement. Stringing a couple hundred of these businesses together gave me leverage with the big manufacturers from whom my clinics would buy their hearing aids—which, by the way, did not include my stepfather's business, spiteful son of a gun that I was.

I used my own wits and brashness to raise the capital I needed to launch Sonus. Then I used my smarts to get Sonus moved from the Alberta, British Columbia, stock exchange to the American Stock Exchange, where I became one of the youngest people ever to ring the opening bell (according to the Exchange), thereby fulfilling at least a version of an early dream I used to have as a kid growing up in Oregon. I even began expanding into Europe, where suppliers were eager to get a foothold in the American hearing aid market in addition to expanding their share in Europe.

Quite the mover and shaker I was—that is, until June of 2002, when the private equity firm I had allowed to acquire a controlling interest in Sonus effectively kicked me out of my own company by bringing in a CEO to sell it. I guess I hated them for it more than I thought, which explained why I kept cursing them and their kind during all those golf outings with Hector. I cursed them even though, looking back at that period from a greater distance of time, I can't say I blamed them one bit. I probably would have done the same thing with the CEO I have come to refer to as "Brandon 1.0."

You see, Brandon 1.0, the old me, exceeded the parameters of his charter as far his ownership partners were concerned. They saw me working deals with manufacturers in Europe that had the potential to create a whole new offshoot of Sonus's business model. That would be great for me, but not so much for them. I had rejected the sound advice of people I admired and respected, who had warned me against this new business for exactly the reason that led the private equity firm to oust me before selling my baby to an international firm for far less than I thought it was worth.

And that's how I ended up with time on my hands and a monolithic chip on my shoulder, pulled over to the side on the ninth, with Hector "LaMarkable" LaMarque delivering me an ultimatum.

What I didn't quite grasp at the time was that while Hector had delivered the ultimatum as a friend who had earned the right to be brutally honest with me, he was offering something more valuable to Brandon 1.0 than friendship. He didn't tell me right away what it was, but I learned that the thing he was offering was mentorship.

People often confuse friendship and mentorship. It's easy to see why. Both involve a close relationship in which one person cares for the other. Like a good friendship, a good mentorship involves mutual respect and a willingness to learn. Like friendship, mentorship requires a great deal of trust from both sides—the mentor must trust in the mentee's earnestness in listening to what he or she has to say and applying it; the mentee must believe that the mentor has his or her best interests in mind and truly wants them to succeed.

But there is a fundamental difference between a friend and a mentor that I had not understood until Hector offered both to me: mentoring is about change. It is about development. You know the old saw about friendship? A friend is someone who knows everything about you . . . *and still likes you.* A mentor is someone who knows everything about you . . . and still likes your chances of becoming something more.

A mentor is someone who you allow to develop you. It would be hard to come up with a relationship, save marriage or parenthood, in which trust matters more than in mentorship. I have enjoyed the support and love of friends and have learned from coaches in both sports and business, but I never thought of them as mentors because they never changed the way I thought about life or behaved toward other people. In some cases I looked for mentors but managed not to notice them, even when they were standing right before my eyes.

Some people might think I was just an independent-minded, self-reliant person, the kind of person a leader ought to be, right? Well, not really—for reasons I'll get to in a minute. The truth is, I never trusted anyone more than I trusted myself. A mentor is someone you have to trust more than yourself. You've got to give up some control and take the action that a mentor recommends out of sheer faith that they have been there and know what to do. Such was the case with Hector—who was also so damn smart that he demanded my respect anyway.

We finished our eighteen holes that day. I wish I could tell you I played the lights out of the back nine, but to tell you the truth, I don't remember a thing about it. What I do remember is that afterward, Hector invited me over to his house for what would become the first mentoring session—well, second, if you count the golf cart incident. He got out a piece of paper and drew a line down the middle of the page.

"Now, what I want you to do is this: in the left-hand column, write down all the remarkable things you've accomplished in your life so far. On the right side, write down all the things which, in assessment, if you had to do them over again, you would do differently."

"Okay, got it," I said.

On the left side, I wrote down how I raised my first million dollars and then my first six million dollars to get Sonus off the ground. I wrote down the moment when I got to ring the opening bell at the American Stock Exchange, then raising my first twenty-eight million. I included acquiring 120 businesses and negotiating global supply agreements. Then, on the right side, I wrote down a considerably longer and more heavily annotated list of "needs improvement" items that included my lack of knowledge about finance and strategic development.

Then I thought about leadership. Was that a strength or a weakness? Well, in all my years of working and leading others, I had formed no meaningful, trusting relationships. I managed by shoving everything down my employees' throats and telling them to "get it done." I could point to very specific instances when wiser heads than mine gave me good advice that I ignored because, hey, I knew better. I was good at making money, so I didn't go to my would-be mentors and ask for their guidance; I felt I had reached a place where I could figure it all out.

Yes, leadership was definitely a right-hand column entry. I made the two lists and handed the page to Hector.

"Now what do I do?" I asked.

"You marked down leadership as a weakness, so read John Maxwell's *The 21 Irrefutable Laws of Leadership*," Hector replied. "You wrote down finance, so read Robert Kiyosaki and Sharon Lechter's book *Cashflow Quadrant*." And then, because my belief system had been so shattered, he told me to read *Beyond Positive Thinking* by Robert Anthony.

Hector not only recommended the books, he went into an adjoining room and brought out copies for me so that I would not leave his house without some homework. That was when I realized that Hector and I had entered into my first ever mentoring relationship. A relationship in which he was saying, "Here are the gaps in your life. Here is what you need to know to fill those gaps. You need to learn it and then apply it."

"My gosh," it dawned on me. "Hector is my first real mentor."

Others had tried to mentor me, including my father and stepfather, but I didn't recognize it as such. Some might say this is the hallmark of a self-made entrepreneur. But I think it was the hallmark of what I have come to call an "entrepreholic." An entrepreholic is someone who forms an addiction to starting businesses that are less and less satisfying and generate smaller and smaller rewards. The condition arises when an entrepreneur has failed to understand their motivation for creating a business in the first place, which often leaves them unsatisfied and restless, even when they "succeed" by making money.

Worse, an entrepreholic rarely learns from mistakes and is doomed to repeat them over and over again, leading to yet more ventures and attempts to finally get it right. In my case, I had been working and earning money, more or less uninterrupted, since I was in fifth grade, living and working by my wits, taking no prisoners, and burning my bridges as I went.

The thing about entrepreholics is that sometimes they play the hero, and sometimes they play the victim. But in either case, they are dominated by fear—fear of failure, fear of a loss of esteem, fear of a lack of control. Name a poison. They also become trapped in an endless rehearsal of the past, which often leads to making bad decisions. During my victim phase, for example, I met a fellow playing golf who wanted to partner with me in business on a project with a billion-dollar upside potential. I was so wrapped up in anger and licking my wounds that I told him I was going to pass. He built the company and sold it for $1 billion in three years.

It would have been the experience of a lifetime to have learned from this man while being part of a billion-dollar sale! But it was just as Hector said: when your thoughts are fixed on what happened in the past, you're not thinking about what you should be doing now and in the future.

So I missed a few great opportunities because I was being a little drainer. No, I missed doing what I was meant to do because I was trying to prove myself to all those people whose names came at the end of those swear words I peppered Hector's ears with. I was a vengeful entrepreholic. Holy smokes! The first thing I'd have to do if I was to break out of this cycle was to discover (or create) a whole new purpose for my future projects.

As I drove away from Hector's house, all I could think was, "Thank God." And thank God I found a mentor who was willing to tell me to shut my mouth and open my mind and figure out where I wanted to go. To bury the past and create the future.

"Go read these books. Find the answers to your questions. Then come back to me," were Hector's parting, Yoda-esque words.

That's exactly what I did.

For additional resources, get immediate access to exclusive behind the scenes videos that uncover even more items I couldn't share in this book. To access these exclusive resources, visit NineFigureTools.com

CHAPTER 2

An Entrepreneur's Beginnings

Are entrepreneurs born or made? People have been arguing about nature versus nurture forever. My experience places me squarely in the nurture camp. My dad was the pastor of a local church and ran a small Christian school as well; my mom was a nurse who specialized in issues relating to hearing loss. They were loving parents who were totally devoted to their kids. My mom's work introduced her to an entrepreneur named Bill Austin, the man who invented the modern hearing aid and went on to found Starkey, which would become one of the world's preeminent makers of hearing aids.

I moved to Minnesota with my mom in 1976 and lived with her and my stepdad during Starkey's start-up years. In 1980 I moved back to Oregon and lived with my dad and my stepmom to finish out middle school and high school. Still, I got to experience the excitement of watching Starkey grow to a $350 million company. When business began booming, my stepdad and mom founded a charitable arm of Starkey called the Starkey Hearing Foundation, which distributed free hearing aids to those who couldn't afford them. Then, a chance conversation put Starkey on the world map and, best of all, I had a role in it.

Representing the foundation, my mom attended a "Just Say No" event in Minneapolis, which was hosted by First Lady of the United States Nancy Reagan, wife of President Ronald Reagan. My mom and Mrs. Reagan started talking, and when the First Lady heard about the family business, she exclaimed, "Oh, my gosh. Ronald can't hear, but he doesn't want people to know." At the time, hearing impairments were stigmatized, and the president believed his would make people think he was old and feeble.

"Well," my mom told Nancy Reagan, "we could fit your husband with a brand-new, state-of-the-art hearing aid that goes inside his ear. People wouldn't even know it was there!"

So my mom and my stepdad went to the president's California ranch to test the president's hearing, take an impression of his ear, and bring the molds back to the factory to have a device custom-made for him. The Reagans wanted to keep it a secret, and I was visiting my mom and stepdad, so I was enlisted as a secret internal courier. I remember walking through the factory holding the president's ear mold and thinking mum was the word. In 1983, they built personalized hearing aids for him, and he wore them for months before a reporter finally asked him what "those things" were in his ear.

"These are my new Starkeys," he said, grinning that well-known grin of his.

Needless to say, after that business became even crazier, and I experienced it firsthand during those summers and holidays when I'd arrive for a stay in town. Visiting my mom and stepdad wasn't about being pampered; it was about learning the hearing aid manufacturing and distribution business from soup to nuts.

Did I take pride in my work and my contribution to the family business? I'm sure I felt some degree of pride, but I also felt a high degree of independence and self-reliance, even as an employee. I was a kid and had to work my share, and there was no other frame of reference that I could relate to. It wasn't so much a case of loving or hating it as it was just doing it because that's what you did.

But working at Starkey during school breaks and summers wasn't the only exposure I had to entrepreneurial endeavors, and one of my earliest took place when I was in high school back in Oregon, where my dad and stepmom had a five-acre walnut orchard on their property. Every year after those walnuts fell, we gathered them up in fifty-pound gunnysacks and sold them out of a little roadside stand. Our revenue goal was $5,500, which paid the tuition to the Christian school I attended.

I used to sit on the tractor and listen to Casey Kasem's *American Top 40* on my little transistor radio, dreaming about the day I would go to New York City to raise money and buy businesses and be a big shot. I told my friends my dreams.

One fall, when I was a high school junior and the year's walnut harvest was due, my parents decided to take a week's vacation together and "empowered" me—that's code for grounding me for breaking curfew—to harvest the year's crop myself. On the Friday they left, I went to school and noticed a flier on one of the lockers announcing that the senior class was holding a fundraising drive to raise $1,000 to finance the senior trip. Necessity is the mother of invention, right? I don't know who said that—either Plato or Frank Zappa—but the president of the senior class was a buddy of mine from the football team, and I asked him if he and a few of the guys on the team would be willing to come out to help me pick up walnuts. I assured him I'd pay them, of course, and they could then use the money to help finance their senior trip.

Little could I have realized that not only would my buddies show up, but also the rest of the senior class and their brothers, sisters, and parents. I found myself managing a hundred people and, just three days later, the orchard was picked cleaner than it had ever been picked before.

"It usually takes us three weeks to finish this job," I told my buddies.

After giving the school the $1,000 to cover the senior trip, I had a $7,700 profit in hand and welcomed my parents back home with the best-looking orchard they'd ever seen in their lives.

"How did you do all this?" was the first question out of my dad's mouth.

I told him all about how, faced with a boring chore, I made a business out of it over a weekend. I proved something to myself and everyone else—that you can meet a big challenge head-on and overcome it. I did that almost effortlessly. Just as important, I became an instant hero among the senior class and my fellow juniors alike. I felt a surge of confidence in my ability to engage other people in my project and see it through to the satisfaction of all concerned. This was a feeling and a skill I would remember and cultivate throughout my life.

I didn't recognize it back then, but looking in the rearview mirror, I see this as an early example of learning that collaborating with other people on a project in which everyone wins is not only possible but also more sustainable and more fun. I learned that the more people you can surround your challenge with, the faster and, if you manage things well, the better you will be able to accomplish things.

At a deeper level, I learned that even if you weren't *nuts* about every aspect of your work—and God knows, I hated harvesting walnuts—you could love the impact that work produces. Lots of people end up hating their jobs because jobs consume precious time and energy, but if you can make your job about something more than the work, you can fall in love with the impact. The parents who came out in the cold and rain to harvest walnuts with their kids didn't care about the money or the price of the trip. They picked and bought the walnuts to show their kids that they loved them.

There was a huge lesson in that insight: the power of purpose.

After high school I began taking classes at Portland State University three days a week. There was a Starkey factory in Portland, so every Wednesday I would go over to the factory and get on the phone to sell hearing aids to distributors. Most entrepreneurs have a zone of genius, the thing they're not only gifted at doing but would do all day even if nobody paid them. My zone of genius was sales. My sales technique was purely instinctive, and it felt easy to just pick up the phone and start talking to people I'd never met.

"Hey, Brandon here," I'd say. "I'm calling from Starkey. Hey, Don, what's your inventory looking like? Do you need more hearing aids?"

Whether they said no or yes, I got into the habit of asking follow-up questions. I might ask them if they had any hearing aids on their shelf and, if they said no, how many they had sold the previous week. If they said four, I'd ask them what would happen if they stocked ten devices rather than their usual quantity of four?

"Do you think you could sell them?" I'd ask.

As often as not, they replied, "Why, yes, Brandon. Yes, I think we would."

Bingo!

And if they expressed concern about excess inventory, I reminded them of Starkey's thirty-day return policy for unused or defective devices, a policy most of the sales reps either forgot about or didn't put in their tool kit during orientation. The upshot was that I regularly sold more hearing aids working one day a week than the full-timers did in five.

My success did not go unnoticed. One day I got a call from my stepdad asking me how life was treating me. I'm sure the savvy businessman in him quickly sussed out that I wasn't exactly thriving in college.

"We're opening another factory in Atlanta and need an outside sales rep," he said. "If you're not excited about staying in school and are as good as you seem to be at sales, I may have an out for you!"

▪ ▪ ▪

We all hoped my creativity and ambition would make an immediate impact on the company's success. I moved to Atlanta, signed out my company car, and started crushing it as far as sales went. I felt free as a bird: nineteen years old with a company car, an expense account, and a sales territory that included eleven states to explore. I quickly became one of the company's top salespeople, selling hearing aids out of the trunk of my car to doctors and holding open house forums to educate prospective customers on Starkey's awesome technology.

And then six months or so into the job, I discovered that my boss in Atlanta was having affairs with women in the office. I confronted him on it and he fired me from my own family's company. I felt I couldn't talk to my mother, since she had only recently found out I wasn't going to college in Portland, and I couldn't face telling her that the job in Atlanta was a bust. I felt my stepdad should be the one calling me rather than taking my boss's word for it. I felt trapped, and so I called no one.

I was out of a job, out of a car, and out of money, and soon I was homeless. But something happened to me in the coming days, weeks, and months that changed my life forever: I learned how to make it on my own. I needed to find some spending money. So I started hustling pool with a dude named Slim, and we started pulling down a few hundred a day. Before long, I met another fellow who sold coupons for discounted services from area businesses to local college students. All of a sudden, between hustling and the advertising gig, I was making more money than I had made at Starkey. For the first time in my life, I could do whatever I wanted to do and didn't have to answer to anyone in the world.

I had another entrepreneurial milestone when I convinced my coupon partner to expand our businesses to include apartment complexes as well as universities. Like universities, apartments brought people to the area who might not be familiar with the local amenities and businesses. These residents lived a short walk from many businesses that we could sell to. Expanding our business in this way taught me about scale and primary and secondary markets, but the larger lesson about scale and innovative technologies came to me when I happened to walk into a video store one day.

Those of you born after 2000 may not know what a video store was. Before people could stream content from their internet connections, they used to rent tapes of movies and television programs at video stores. There were mom-and-pop stores and larger chains, the most successful of which included Blockbuster and Hollywood Video. I remember going into a mom-and-pop store one day and asking the owner how he competed against the chains.

"Do you know that for every three copies of a new movie release you have on your shelves, Blockbuster has something like fifty copies?" I asked. "And did you know they don't even have to pay for the videos? They're so big, they get them for free and just pay the distributors a percentage of what they rent."

The "pop" brushed off my questions by arguing that customer loyalty made up for lack of scale. Over time, even after I left Atlanta, I watched as the mom-and-pop stores were displaced by the big chains, and the big chains were displaced by streaming. There was no way a little business owner could compete against large scale, innovative business models that allowed for rapid scaling, technology advancements, and marketing leverage at unprecedented levels.

I've never stopped thinking about that period, and over the course of my career have spent millions of dollars researching the whole cycle of mom-and-pop stores to big-box stores to streaming services, like Netflix. The cycle took about twenty years. This might seem like a long time, but it went by in the blink of an eye. Even now, in my presentations to businesses, I draw on what I learned walking Atlanta's Jimmy Carter Boulevard: Don't get so focused and comfortable with your situation that you forget to expand and innovate. If you don't expand and innovate, you will eventually be out of business.

After about three weeks, my stepdad called to tell me he wanted to bring me back to Starkey, but I was having so much fun knocking it out of the park in Atlanta that I said no. Then, after six months in

Atlanta, the boss who fired me was himself fired for sexual harassment, which led to my receiving another call from my stepdad asking me to reconsider coming back into the fold, this time as his assistant sales manager in Minneapolis, Minnesota. I felt totally vindicated and, since I wanted to advance up the ladder at Starkey, agreed to return.

But I also remember feeling that although I was going back to work with my stepdad, I would always be able to take care of myself. I didn't have to depend on the whims of another person.

▪ ▪ ▪

Although my second stint at Starkey, which began in 1989, put my entrepreneurial ambitions on hold for a while longer, I did use the period to serve in an "intrapreneurial" capacity. This became most obvious in my taking over Starkey's promotional cruise for our loyal and premium customers. The goal was to thank our customers for their loyalty while incentivizing them to remain loyal by enrolling them in new programs. The director of sales who had previously over- seen this project had failed to produce enough future sales commit- ments to finance the cruise, so my stepdad put me in charge of firing the sales director and running the project.

I had an idea of how to do it, which involved printing coupon books the sales reps could give to their customers for discounts on hearing aids, and I raised the price on the devices themselves just a bit. Within ninety days and with a month to spare, we raised the additional money needed to fund the cruise. I had succeeded in spec- tacular fashion but made no friends in the process—I had a little bit of a reputation for firing my boss, and none of the VPs were big fans of mine.

I can't deny that I was a brash and tenacious son of a gun. As I had done in Atlanta, I seemed to be absolutely crushing it from a sales perspective. For the next year's promotional cruise, I raised the sales goal from $4 million to $12 million through the use of my coupon program. As in the previous year, we met our target by raising prices on new products that our customers were signing on to purchase.

While I was busy making money and burning bridges back at headquarters, my mom and stepdad began a lengthy divorce process that I managed to get in the middle of. I won't belabor the whole thing—this is a business book, not a soap opera—but the long story short of it is that I realized Starkey was not going to be a place where I could pursue my dreams and ambitions of making something of myself *and making something of my own.*

So I made a decision. I told my stepdad I wanted to talk to him one night and I told him what I was going to do.

"I'm quitting, effective immediately," I said. "I'm selling everything, including the brand-new house we bought, and I'm moving to Oregon to start my life over."

I would leave with my wife, my two year old, and my newborn, and I wouldn't look back. He tried to convince me to reconsider, but I'd tasted a delicious brand of independence in Atlanta, and it suited me. It was 1995 and I was twenty-seven years old, and if I felt I knew anything at all about myself, it was that I could do it all again—and even better this time.

Atlanta had changed my life forever. Now, I was going to draw on that same resilience and confidence to do it again—this time in Oregon.

For additional resources, get immediate access to exclusive behind the scenes videos that uncover even more items I couldn't share in this book. To access these exclusive resources, visit NineFigureTools.com

CHAPTER 3

Creating My Own Company

The way I saw it, I was twenty-seven years old when I quit being an employee and began my journey to being an owner. I had enough money to live on for six or seven months after I sold my house and moved to Oregon. On the plus side, I had an idea for a new business model even before I quit Starkey.

When I was at the company, I had noticed that the hearing care industry was going through a change; audiology clinics were moving from being owned by business-minded operators to being owned by highly trained professionals, often with medical degrees. The older generation of business owners had no clear exit strategy, nor were they flush with money. The newly educated practitioners were talented technicians, but they weren't businesspeople. Plus, they were coming out of school with debt. I saw a huge and exciting opportunity to buy those existing businesses and hire the next generation of providers to work for me. I would be the first in the industry to do this.

I had wanted to start a new division at Starkey called Financial Management Services to deal with this shift in our marketplace. When I told the higher-ups at Starkey, however, they told me that owning the companies we sold to was a conflict of interest. I disagreed. When I decided to leave Starkey, I thought, "Fine, I'll create the network on my own!"

I resigned on December 15, 1995, and launched my new business in February of 1996. In February, I met a businessman named Doug Good who was married to a hearing care business owner in Vancouver. Doug wanted to consolidate Canada's hearing care market, but he and his wife also wanted to retire. The job of running his business turned out to be more difficult and tedious than he had expected, and he was looking for a way to take his foot off the pedal. I convinced him to sell me half of his company—even though I didn't have enough money to buy it.

Doug wanted to spend more time on the golf course, and I managed to convince him that if he sold me half of his business on a long-term note, the other half he owned would eventually be worth more than the whole. He could play golf and I could pursue my vision of consolidating audiology clinics.

By April, I had run out of money and realized that my dream might go up in smoke unless I could get the funding needed to make it happen. I had to find an investor who would front $1 million that I could put into the company, and that meant a whole lot of legwork. During the two months that followed, Doug and I made twenty-three presentations to potential investors, without any success.

At 10 p.m. on the night before we were to make our twenty-fourth presentation, I found myself on a foggy, icy stretch of Interstate 5, driving from Portland, Oregon, to Vancouver, British Columbia, for a meeting that had the potential to make or break me. If the meeting went the way I hoped, I could carry out my plan of buying audiology clinics and obtain security and peace of mind for my young family. If I didn't, the future posed nothing but a question mark. I was careening blindly into the void. As I looked deep into the fog, focusing my eyes on the lines on either side of the road, the unknown outcomes in my head were loud and relentless.

At midnight, overcome with emotion, I pulled off the highway and sobbed. I hadn't cried like that since I was eight years old when my mother and father divorced, but the feeling was much too familiar. The self-assured, fast-talking, fast-thinking, full-of-life man I had become quickly transported back in time. I became a little boy again, and I was scared, full of doubt, insecure, and terrified about the future.

And yet in spite of my dark mood, another part of me felt confident that this next phrase was going to work. After all, I had experienced a sudden change of life plans several years earlier in Atlanta and emerged from the ordeal not only surviving but thriving. Whatever the next chapter threw at me, I'd nail that too.

That knowledge lifted my spirits as I crossed the Canadian border. I pulled into Vancouver a little before 4 a.m. To stay awake, I downed several cups of coffee from a gas station and psyched myself up for our early morning meeting. It worked. I went into that meeting smelling the millions. I pulled out my gray suit, a two-button Armani I had reclaimed from Nordstrom Rack, buttoned my white Calvin Klein shirt, and made a medium knot in my black-and-white striped tie. I took one last look in the mirror. I was ready.

At one point in our presentation, I sensed Doug had lost our potential investor's attention, so I made a bold move and interrupted. Looking directly at the potential investor, I got to the point: "If you just trust me with a million dollars, I will prove to you why and how this will work."

The potential investor looked at me and said, "Why should I trust you?" It was certainly a fair question, but my response caught him off guard.

"Because in order for you to get good returns for your investors on their money," I said, "you have to invest the money. Every investment is a risk, but in your situation, even if you make a few bad investments, you can offset them with one or two great investments. It's different for me. I only have this one chance to make my dreams come true, and if it doesn't work, I will be viewed as a failure."

I went on to tell them that this was my big chance to establish my credibility for the rest of my life. I had no choice but to make it work. Wouldn't they rather invest in someone with a diehard mindset than someone who just wanted to make it happen?

"From where I'm sitting," I concluded, "I'm the most secure investment risk you will ever make, because I won't give up until I succeed."

The potential investor stared at me, slack-jawed, obviously stunned that I was speaking so honestly. I used the silence that ensued to my advantage, pressing harder and proposing to him that if he told me what time he finished work the next day, I'd pick him and drive him over to the business I planned to buy.

"I'll show you the economics, the capital requirements, the psychology of the sellers, and my operating plan. Give me the chance to prove why this opportunity is a surefire winner. Trust me, and I won't fail you."

Although the potential investor's broker jumped in to remind me that I was a guest and shouldn't be so pushy, and Doug and Hugh looked like they wanted to jump across the table and throttle me, the potential investor stared at me with a look in his eyes that I recognized. A look of *respect*.

Taking my cues from Doug and Hugh, I apologized for being aggressive. I assured them that it hadn't been my intention to be disrespectful to them or anyone in the meeting, but that I had nothing to lose. I was taking a risk for a goal we all shared. The potential investor looked at me for what seemed an eternity. Then he stood up and reached out to shake my hand. He asked me to meet him in front of his building the next day at 4 p.m. sharp . . . *alone*.

After returning to my hotel that night, I was sweating bullets and hardly slept a wink. With very little rest, I woke up the next morning knowing the day would either be the beginning of my future or the end of my dream. We had exhausted our list of investor options. It was my last chance not only to inspire my vision but also to show

Doug and Hugh that my intuition was correct, that my plan was worth $1 million.

I picked up the potential investor at 4 p.m. sharp, drove him to the location of the business, and showed him the details of the audiology practice and financials. On the way back, he challenged me with one question after another: "What makes you think you can do this? How will it work?"

Without hesitation, I was able to answer every one of his questions and he appeared impressed with my confidence and knowledge. I dropped him off at his building, looking for him to say yes. He said he would think about it.

"Trust me," I said, with every fiber of conviction in my body, "and I promise you that you'll never lose your money."

At nine o'clock that evening, Doug's phone rang, and the potential investor invited us to his house for a drink. Doug, Hugh, and I showed up forty-five minutes later, and as the investor poured us some wine, he handed me an envelope. In it was a check for $1 million. I'd never held a check for $1 million before. The feeling was indescribable. For an instant, it brought about an out-of-body experience as fear mixed with total elation washed over me in the moment I had begun visualizing when I was a kid. The resilience I'd developed in Atlanta sealed the deal.

But I soon came back down to earth. *It was time to get to work.*

▪ ▪ ▪

The company that Doug Good sold me went public and was listed on the Alberta Canada Stock Exchange. I had no idea how to run a public company as the CEO, so I had to learn, and learn fast, from Good. He started teaching me about the public markets and about governance, fiduciary responsibilities, and duties—things you would not know unless you had taken a business public before, which I hadn't. Part of my responsibilities included quarterly presentations to financial analysts and discussing the numbers as though I understood them.

Looking back, Doug was really one of my first mentors on how to properly and responsibly run a company. It was crazy, but it was so much fun because I was living a version of my dream of being a player—the guy I'd dreamt about becoming back in that walnut orchard in Oregon.

When I bought 50 percent of Doug's interest, the stock was selling for eight cents a share. Within a year of my running the business, its stock rose to a dollar, so I owned $9 million of value in the business. That's when I discovered something else about public companies: I could use my stock holdings like a currency with which to buy new audiology clinics and consolidate my business. Before long, I had bought up three audiology clinics whose owners were retiring. I kept on visiting more and more clinics and, while I couldn't buy them all, I secured letters of intent that added up to $20 million.

After I got that first million, Doug introduced me to his investment banking friends in Dallas: Marc Still, Baron Cass, and John Strauss. I met with them over the course of several months and built a more trusting, personal relationship with them. I also joined Marc on business trips to New York to talk with other potential investors about the prospect of what "could be done." That was investment-speak for "showing Brandon the money."

The New Yorkers issued me a challenge.

"If you can get $15–$20 million worth of business at your current pricing structure to sell out to you, we'll invest $6 million into your company for the cash required to buy them," they told me. In just nine short months, I was able to get all the required businesses under a letter of intent to sell. The total agreed to was $20 million. In December of 1996, Marc, Baron, and John wired me the $6 million, and I closed on the businesses.

Flush with new energy, confidence, and the $6 million they had wired me, I succeeded in getting another $100 million in businesses under letters of intent. This success prompted a need for more capital, so we headed to New York to make presentations to private equity groups. We must have made seventy-five presentations, the majority of which ended with us being laughed out of the office or being told that given my age and lack of experience, nobody would trust me with that much money. Once again, I turned to Marc for some badly needed coaching. All of a sudden, I started getting bids. The big moment came when I presented to Warburg Pincus, one of the largest and most prestigious financial private equity groups in the "club" at the time with around $14 billion under management.

In my presentation, I asked for $15 million. They listened, then told me they would talk and get back to me. Three weeks later they called and did something that completely took me by surprise: they offered $18 million.

"Why would you do that?" I asked them.

"Giving you $18 million instead of $15 million will allow you to meet the listing requirement to move your company off the Alberta Stock Exchange and list it on the American Stock Exchange," they explained.

And so I delisted from Canada and listed in the United States, and, in February of 1998, at the age of twenty-nine, became one of the (or *the*!) youngest ever to ring the opening bell on the American Stock Exchange. I had $100 million in intent-to-sell business lined up. From this perspective, I was sitting on the top of the world.

But I had a problem—I didn't have anything close to the kind of team I needed to manage the businesses. I needed a "deal" team to wine and dine prospective owners, perform due diligence, and close the deals; I needed an "integrations" team to recharge the businesses whose owners had essentially stopped working once they saw retirement looming; and I needed an innovation team because I had to build systems, processes, teams, and technologies to manage all these companies I was acquiring.

My company, US Sonus Hearing Centers—*sonus* is Latin for "sound"—had clinics in California, the Pacific Northwest, Canada, and in the Midwest around Chicago, because I bought some larger offices that had numerous locations. As I grew my business, I found myself tying up millions in acquiring the clinics—but unable to persuade their managers to do daily cash deposits. Yikes. I needed more money to build new technology to improve my receivables. As a public company, I needed real-time reporting.

So I acquired a receivables business that was an expert at collecting third-party payables, and we started having all of our clinics ship their bills there overnight. There, the money would be billed and collected. The problem was that the owners of the company checked out right after we acquired them and my CFO was not paying attention and managing them, therefore five months of billing and collecting didn't get done, leaving boxes and boxes of unpaid bills piling up, and all of my cashflow sitting dead on the shelves.

One day my CFO walked in and said, "We can't make payroll."

When I asked why, he said the third-party company wasn't collecting any of the managed care money. I immediately fired the owners of the company and took all the bills back to our home office. In reflection, this was probably the biggest learning moment in my life: at the end of the day, I was the one responsible for making sure my CFO and the owners we acquired did their job, and this is where I learned that abdication is not a leadership quality and can be quite costly! As a business owner, I did what too many owners do and allowed myself to get spread too thin and wide, assuming that my teams were going to stay on top of things. There were a million little checks I could have done to ensure this didn't happen, but I didn't do any of them.

Losing time and money weren't the only negative consequences of my mistake.

In 1999, I did an emergency round of financing for $10 million with Warburg Pincus to solve the huge cash flow problem we were facing. Within the next six months, we solved that problem, but in doing so set up another longer-term problem I would live to regret: in getting this next round of financing, I gave Warburg Pincus the controlling interest in my company.

Soon after, I heard from suppliers of hearing aids in Germany and Denmark and other parts of Europe that they were seeing the same wave of retirements in their marketplaces that I had recognized in North America. Germany alone had thirty locations. Much as I had been, the Danish manufacturing companies were concerned about losing customers to retirement. Would I be willing to accept a loan from them to buy the clinics at zero percent interest, with the proviso that I would steer their business in the right direction?

I said yes and proceeded to integrate the new companies into the Sonus network, all the while strengthening the network by offering even better buying power and creating better operational efficiencies, not least around accounts receivable, which many of the Sonus members had been far too lax with. Not anymore.

I felt good about where we were heading. But I had missed one critical mistake. I had been solving problems right and left, making money and moving so fast that I made the enormous error of not listening to my board, which included majority shareholders, when they told me they didn't like the model. Specifically, they didn't like the debt I was going to incur from the German and Danish suppliers. Even though the financing was interest-free, that's not what the board had signed on for. They told me that if I wanted to do deals like that, I should consider setting up a separate company. The board of directors informed me they would be happy to give me a waiver to do so.

I thought, briefly, about checking in with Marc and my buddies in Texas to get their read on the situation, but ultimately I trusted my own instincts. I went ahead and made arrangements to receive a $20 million interest-free loan from the Danish supplier and immediately took the business's profits from zero to over $1 million a month. I was so giddy with growth that when a German manufacturer came to me and told me he wanted me to buy out its customers and give that manufacturer all of the business—for another cool $20 million in interest-free loan money—I told him about my conditions for doing business with me, as I'd told everyone else.

Pretty cool, huh?

I certainly thought so . . . at the time. Even my board told me I had pulled off the most creative financing they'd ever seen. The Danish company loved the deal, too, and showed its gratitude in advance of closing by booking my wife and me on the Orient Express for a two-week meet-and-greet European vacation. If you had sat across from me in the dining car and asked me, "Brandon, at precisely what point in your career did you know that you had finally arrived?" I would have smiled and said, "Right now. Right here on this train!"

It was May of 2001. With a new business line generating more than $1 million of pure profit a month and a credit line of $20 million advanced to me with zero interest, I was about to be swimming in cash and, if I was totally and completely honest, probably well on my way to becoming one of those billionaires I had known back at the golf club. When I landed back in the US, the board of directors asked me to come to New York for a meeting.

"A congratulations meeting, no doubt," I thought, feeling like the twenty million bucks I had gotten from the Danish supplier.

The meeting did not go as I expected.

"Now that you've raised that $20 million—and great financing, by the way, the most creative we've ever seen—the money is technically debt on the books, isn't it?" they asked. "We told you not to create the network program, but you did it anyway, and now you're selling distressed assets with the money we invested in the company. This makes the money debt on the books, and because it's debt on the books, we're selling the business."

"Come on, guys!" I said. "This is total BS! We're finally making money. We've got free capital and we're going to dominate the marketplace on a global basis. Everything we've worked for is ready to start taking off, and you guys are telling me you're gonna sell the business? That's the dumbest thing I've ever heard. I'm not selling the business."

That didn't move them one bit.

"We bought a company with no debt," the board members told me. "And if we calculate what we invested, and what we could sell the company for today, we'd get all our money back, plus we would get all our preferred internal returns before anyone else got anything. We don't want you to take any of that money because then you and your manufacturing buddies will have leverage on us. So the upshot is that we want you to sell the business."

Sell the business? Sell this thing I had practically built from scratch with my own wits and energy? I snickered at them and told them there was not a chance in hell.

"Every CEO says that," was their reply.

They brought in a CEO from the next room and said, "Dan is replacing you." They effectively fired me, kicking me upstairs to the chairman of board, and sold the company. At the time, I was mad as hell, but I look back now and realize that I learned a very expensive lesson about capital structures. And if I'm being truly honest with myself, I can't say I blame the private equity people for doing what they did. Making money was their job, not making lifelong friends. I would have done the same thing. They warned me against doing it and I went ahead and did it anyway because *I thought I knew better*. I changed the game on them midstream and did things differently than I said I would.

Once again, I was on my own and starting over, only this time I had enough money to lick my wounds from the vantage of a golf cart at a posh club. And this brings us back to the beginning, with Hector laying down the law to me about taking ownership of the pattern my life seemed to have taken, a pattern of success followed by self-sabotage and feeling victimized. This kind of life, averred Hector, was no kind of life at all, and I knew it was time for this college dropout to go back to school.

My campus: the University of Hector.

For additional resources, get immediate access to exclusive behind the scenes videos that uncover even more items I couldn't share in this book. To access these exclusive resources, visit NineFigureTools.com

CHAPTER 4

Hector Sends Me
Back to School

After Hector and I had our come-to-Jesus encounter on
the golf course, I decided to take a sabbatical to figure out how to
write the next chapter of my life so it wouldn't turn out exactly like all
the previous chapters. One thought kept resonating with me. It was
something Hector had told me that day on the golf course.

"You're stuck. And until you get unstuck, you cannot move forward with your life."

That was where I had to begin—by getting unstuck. I realized I
was stuck because I had never decided what I wanted to make of my
life. I was a born-and-bred worker and doer. I knew that. And I had
always wanted to run my own business. I knew that too. But why
had I wanted these things? The answer, I realized, seemed insepara-
ble from my need to prove myself to other people, specifically to my
mom and stepdad. If I was to be the rightful heir to the great Starkey
throne, I felt I had to impress them—and everyone else—with my
intelligence and ability to get results. While at Starkey, I let nothing
and no one get in my way, and sometimes I stepped on people as I
climbed the ladder of success.

Quitting Starkey and starting Sonus ended my dream of one day running the family business, but it did little to change my fundamental mindset. I ran Sonus with the same lack of awareness of others, believing I was smarter and shrewder than everyone else. As with Starkey, my success in building Sonus from nothing to a $70 million company only reinforced my arrogance, so that when my investors asked me *not* to do something, I did it anyway.

That's not confidence. It's arrogance. Confidence is a belief in yourself; arrogance is a belief *only* in yourself.

I couldn't get past using Sonus as a platform to prove to the world (and to myself) that I could do it. It proved to me that I was a winner and, just as important, not a loser. Not the guy who had graduated high school with a lousy grade point average, dropped out of college, gotten fired from his family's company, and then gotten fired from his own company. No one cared that I had made Sonus successful, because I hadn't brought them along on the journey. The journey had been all about Brandon, all about me. And looking back, how else could I possibly have expected my life to have turned out up to that point?

I had been the boss, but I had never become a leader. This is what undermined my success. So the first thing I had to figure out was . . . what did I want? What was my dream? Fortunately, I had a noncompete clause with Sonus to keep me grounded and enough money to take a year or so to figure out the ideal scenario for the rest of my life.

MY MAXWELL HOMEWORK

The good news was that Hector already knew what I didn't—and far more importantly, what I did not know that I did not know—and gave me exactly the right books to read. The first was John Maxwell's *21 Irrefutable Laws of Leadership*. Early in the book, Maxwell outlines some of the characteristics of true leaders. I was happy to see that I recognized some of those traits in myself. These included "ability," "experience," and "knowledge," all traits I felt I had in abundance.

But there were several in which I was completely lacking, and they were the ones Maxwell obviously prized the most. Heading the list was the quality of relationships. Here's what Maxwell has to say: "You're a leader only if you have followers, and that always requires the development of relationships—the deeper the relationships, the stronger the potential for leadership." Had I attracted followers beyond those who followed me to get a paycheck? Were they followers who admired and trusted my character and intuition about life and work? More to the point, had I done much to encourage the people I did influence to believe in the projects I valued and to which I wanted them to devote their energy and time?

I had to admit the answer was no.

In the chapter "The Law of Magnetism," I learned that who we attract to our projects is based not on what we want, but on who we are. If a person's inner world is dominated by a monolithic ax he's grinding, an old score he could never quite settle, or a desperate need to prove himself, he will attract similar people. If such is the case, then all the experience and the most polished skill set in the world won't change a person's attitude. Thinking back on Sonus, it occurred to me that if I thought the clinic owners I'd bought out weren't putting their whole souls into their businesses after I'd bought them, I had to look in the mirror and ask myself just how much I was committed to their success. I was committed to my own success, that was for sure. But how could I expect to succeed without bringing others along with me?

And then I considered Maxwell's "The Law of the Lid," which states that "personal and organizational effectiveness are proportional to leadership." Maxwell illustrates the law using the example of Dick and Maurice McDonald, the brothers who invented the fast-food restaurant that still bears their name. Although the brothers invented the concept for the world's most scalable restaurant, their challenge was that they could not imagine scalability. They were too limited in their thinking and leadership skills to imagine operating more than the ten locations they managed to open.

And then a fellow named Ray Kroc came along, who was an entirely different kind of businessman, one who had a grand vision of how big the brothers' unique offering might become. Kroc entered into partnership with them, eventually bought them out, and went full speed ahead with creating the world's most successful franchise.

The McDonalds' leadership capacity—their lid, as Maxwell would say—tapped out at ten locations. Kroc's leadership lid blew the hinges off the structure. Between 1955 and 1959, Kroc opened 100 McDonald's restaurants. Four years later, there were 500 of them, and today there are 38,000 McDonald's worldwide and counting. Kroc was undoubtedly a better operator, one who understood how to scale systems and processes to guarantee quality and cut wasted steps. This was how he was able to bring each new McDonald's online as a lean, mean burger-flipping machine. But the operational effectiveness and leadership quality he demonstrated arose from a single source: his unlimited belief that the world would share his love for "the beauty of a hamburger" that looked and tasted the same everywhere it was served.

So many of my formative years in business pitted me against the world—in a zero-sum game that produced only winners and losers—that I was unprepared to digest another one of Maxwell's laws, at least at first. "The Law of Addition" sounded bland enough, but there was nothing bland about its implications for thinking about what kind of leader I might aspire to become. "The bottom line in leadership," Maxwell's law says, "isn't how far we advance ourselves but how far we advance others." Nothing about the way businesses competed against each other for customers or the way investors viewed companies they put money into convinced me that advancing others played much of a role in whose bank account grew the most. It was a dog-eat-dog world, as far as I could tell.

But now, reading Maxwell's book, what jumped out at me was the idea that I could choose what kind of world I wished to live in.

And that began by deciding what kind of professional relationships I wanted to have as a leader.

"The interaction between every leader and follower is a relationship, and all relationships either add to or subtract from a person's life," Maxwell writes. "If you are a leader, then trust me, you are having either a positive or a negative impact on the people you lead."

Maxwell's critical question: "Are you making things better for the people who follow you?"

Had I made things better for the people who had followed me? I supposed some would say so, while others would say not. But that question wasn't entirely on point, for the simple reason I had never thought about it as the province of leadership. Beyond giving merit raises and bonuses or promotions, I had always thought of leadership as being in charge, building a great company, improving an organization's processes and systems, and beating the competition. It hurts a little to admit now, but more often than not, I found my employees to be obstacles to accomplishments rather than allies. And the more I thought about it, the more it occurred to me that I had set up my business to undermine my best efforts.

THE UNIVERSITY OF HECTOR

My visits to Hector's sales presentations at Primerica had impressed me so much that I wanted to see whether our mentoring relationship could include some in-depth, one-on-one coaching. Hector had a beautiful house in Balboa Island, Newport Beach. I asked him if I could prepare a list of questions for him and videotape his answers. I mean, that's what mentors did, right? The person being mentored came with questions and the mentor answered them as best as he or she could. I had an absolute master of salesmanship and leadership offering his mentorship to me, so I wanted to absorb as much as I could—not just in the moment but also to use later. Some people prefer to take notes on paper; I learn better by hearing and seeing something, so the videos made the most sense to me.

I scheduled five hours for us and set up the video camera facing him in his living room and just began throwing questions at him, one after the other. I decided that the best approach was to be as granular as I possibly could; my goal was not only to listen to his answers but also to understand his thought process. That was the real value in our sessions, and a lesson I would pass along to others. The goal in a mentoring relationship doesn't end with finding answers to your questions; the greatest gain comes from understanding how a master thinks and why he or she thinks that way.

"If you met someone for the first time, what would you do? What would you say?" I asked. And then he told me.

"If you met somebody you were trying to recruit to work on your team at Primerica, and they told you they weren't happy in their current job, what would you say to engage them and make them curious about what they could do on your team?"

I had a host of questions along this line and just kept going.

"How would you recruit somebody to come to work in your organization?"

"What would you say to them?"

"How would you talk about how the compensation works?"

"What would you tell them about how you're going to help them actually learn the business?"

"What are the top three frustrations of your current job?"

"What are you willing to invest in to eliminate those frustrations and earn the kind of money you want and have the life you want?"

Hector's answers took me through the entire process of painting a clear picture of success and making it easy for people to see their own success inside what you'd done in your business.

"The leader's job is to make other people's success easy to picture. The way you recruit people is to identify what's important to them personally, professionally, and financially and get them to talk about what they are not able to accomplish in their present circumstance. And then you explain what you do in your organization to allow people to set their goals and actually achieve them and be successful."

That's the magic that I went on to use in each of my businesses.

When we were finished, I planned on taking the tape to a videographer I knew and asking him to edit the narrative into about thirty-five definitive Hector nuggets that I could use to train people when, someday, I created my new company. I continued to ask Hector questions for a couple of weeks. During this time, I learned another lesson: the quality of your questions determines the quality of your answers. If you work hard to craft the best questions you can—making lists of questions and constantly revising them, deleting those that don't lead anywhere—you will gain much more insight and value.

The first thing anyone should ask themselves before approaching someone to mentor them is how they would like to spend their time. In fact, most mentors who are highly sought after ask this very question to weed out the unfocused. I used to spend as much time as I could, thinking as granularly as I could, in order to ask as many questions as I was permitted to squeeze in before my mentor grew exhausted. The goal was an understanding of not only what they did, but also what they were thinking about as they put their plans into action. I wanted to know what kinds of goals they formulated and how they measured their results. If they had built a billion-dollar business, what was the first thing they did, the second thing, and so on until I understood the full context of their success. I would rather go deep into one area than broadly into several.

This technique yielded a lot of gold from Hector, but one nugget that stood out then, and still stands out today, as a game-changer in my thinking involved his idea of scaling a business. He referred to it by the acronym 3M, which stood for "model, mimic, and mastery."

MODEL, MIMIC, MASTER, AND MULTIPLY

We were talking about building leadership capacity in a business going through rapid growth when Hector paused for a moment and said, "Dude, there's no point doing anything after you master it. After you master something, your next step is teaching other people how to do it, and then teaching them how to teach others, because there's no leverage in doing anything on a one-to-one ratio."

Every year, Gallup does a massive survey of US employee attitudes and, nearly every year, it says that two-thirds of the workers feel disengaged from their work and 18 percent are "actively" disengaged, which means they are trying to subvert the company that employs them. The subversion could range from a little bit of deliberate time wasting here and there or not giving it their all, to bad-mouthing the employer in public or even stealing! On the surface, such behavior seems ungrateful at best and pathological at worst. But reading Maxwell, a switch flipped in my brain and I began to see how purely transactional relationships could serve to "lower the lid" on employee motivation and ethical behavior.

Maxwell's "Law of Addition" argues that adding value to others over time creates a multiplier effect that benefits both those whom the leader serves and the leader as well. The way this works is that when you add value to an employee, you lift them up, inspire them, advance their career, and make them feel like a vested participant in something bigger. You help them achieve their dreams and become the best version of themselves. As a business owner, who would I rather entrust my precious baby to: someone who feels personally, professionally, and financially invested in our project's success, or someone who lives the vast majority of their workdays waiting for paychecks and weekends?

The problem I faced at Sonus, Hector argued, was that even when I managed to turn it into a $70 million company, I was still finding the deals, negotiating the deals, raising the money to close the deals, and overseeing the payroll process—basically everything having to do with running the company.

"You never built a team around you that could multiply the knowledge and actions needed to expand," Hector said. "You shouldn't be adding people if you're not intending on multiplying *through* people."

Using the multiplier effect, you should add people who are crystal clear about where they fit in the organization and what you expect from them. Then you teach them to do that with the people below them. And that becomes the discipline in the organization. The leader creates the model and teaches others how to mimic the model. That said, it is not enough to have everyone in your company mimicking thought and behavior if they don't understand what they're doing, right? That's where mastery enters the picture. Once you have a culture in which people are mimicking all the right things, you need to designate some of your exceptional people to become masters of the model themselves so they can continue the multiplier effect.

"This is why my Primerica way works," Hector told me, which made sense since it was a multi-level marketing model.

But why, I wondered, *couldn't it work in a more traditional business setting as well?* The hurdle in traditional businesses arose from the tendency for leaders to view knowledge and know-how as precious assets that add to their own power. For this reason, they were often reluctant to share what they knew and how they did what they did with those for whom they were responsible. This accounted for the largely defensive posture that slowed companies down rather than sped them up as they grew. But what if the leader's main responsibility was not to protect his or her position but to ensure that the entire organization was executing effectively on mimicking and mastering the models he or she had set out to guide everybody in the first place? I mean, they would still be driving strategies, right?

When I opened my next company, I followed this line of thinking with the first person I hired. When we first started doing cold calling, for example, he would watch me and listen to how I talked to prospective customers. After doing this for a while, we would do these kinds of joint calls where he would initiate the conversation with the customer, and I would be available to jump in and add some important information or get the customer to make a decision to progress forward. We'd listen to transcripts and talk about it for a while, and then he'd be in charge of the whole call. After doing this for a while, he was able to draw on our video people to create his own training videos, freeing me from having to train anyone on sales calls ever again. I could move on to other things. Lesson learned.

LISTEN LIKE A STUDENT

Hector was always very complimentary of me when it came to my eagerness to listen and learn from others. Not everyone who has successfully created their own $70 million business is humble enough to admit he doesn't have all the answers—but I had some things going for me. I wasn't overly educated, to put it mildly, so I never got locked into the kinds of thinking systems they taught at school, particularly business school.

When I was selling hearing aids as a twenty year old in Atlanta, I didn't have a particularly in-depth command of the technical side of how hearing aids worked. The only hearing test results I understood amounted to normal hearing and then mild, moderate, and severe hearing loss. When people came in to drop off their test results, they would chat with us, and unlike the more technically trained sales reps who could explain the features of our devices right down to the smallest widget, I figured out how to turn the conversation around.

When someone walked in, I'd ask what brought them in here today.

"Well, we've been fighting about how loud the TV is at our house," they'd say, or, "We've been fighting because I think my wife mumbles and we can't go out anymore because we just can't hear."

And I would ask them, "If we could solve that problem, would you want to experience what that would be like?"

And they'd say, "You bet we would. Let's do it."

"Okay, let's see what we can do."

Based on the test results and this perfectly nontechnical conversation, I could sell them hearing aids. It was a whole lot easier than attempting to learn the science of hearing loss. Sometimes, asking good questions offers a much better way of relating to people than making statements at them—especially if you don't know what it is you're talking about. That openness to learning was the quality that had impressed Hector about me, more than any claims I might have made about my accomplishments or work ethic. Part of my education at the University of Hector involved understanding not only how other successful, intelligent people thought, *but also how I thought*. If you don't understand how you think and why you believe the things you do, I reasoned, how could you possibly know what you needed to change about your thoughts and beliefs? In many ways, this was the greatest gift of all that came out of those sabbatical years.

For additional resources, get immediate access to exclusive behind the scenes videos that uncover even more items I couldn't share in this book. To access these exclusive resources, visit NineFigureTools.com

CHAPTER 5

Engineering a New Kind of Business

During my sabbatical, I began doing research on merger and acquisition companies and noted that many had failed between 1997 and 2003, even though when I studied their market analysis and financial modeling, it seemed like they should have been hugely successful. Why would this be? My "aha!" moment seized me by the collar when I recalled my own experience acquiring mom-and-pop businesses at Sonus. Even when a company looked good on paper, its success still depended on the emotional connection and alignment of the people in the acquired businesses who had to do the work.

There are a couple of different strategies. One is a "roll-up" strategy, in which you buy other people's businesses and consolidate them. The other is the franchisor-franchisee model, where the franchisor tells the franchisee what they can or cannot do. I call both of these "cram-down models" because somebody else is dictating how you build your business. To use the consolidation version, if you're a seller who has been underperforming and suddenly begins performing well after being bought, you might get angry because in your mind the buyer must have known there was more potential than you realized.

In addition, you're seeing how much more money the buyer is making and are feeling like you sold too cheap. You may feel that you're not getting a fair share of the money and more upside.

If this sounds rather unpleasant for the seller, well, that's because it largely is.

As I talked to other consolidators, I asked them to give me their impressions of where things had gone sideways. Their answers led to an epiphany involving the psychology of the seller or buyer or franchisor-franchisee relationship. I recalled my meetings with Warburg Pincus and how the smart young analysts would tell me, "The numbers never lie. If the franchisees or business owners aren't hitting their numbers, it's their fault." The problem with this line of thinking was that it didn't help me understand what I might do to change things for a low-producing company I'd bought. How might a franchisee or independent business owner go about attracting, developing, and retaining remarkable people in order to get the numbers to actually work?

I also heard other investors state that they didn't invest in business concepts but in leadership teams. So where was the conversation about talent acquisition and management in all of this mumbo jumbo about the numbers never lying?

I put these different strands of thought together and asked myself how I could create a business system that pulled people up rather than shoved them into a box—a business system that created value for the business owners and their teams and the consolidation company or franchise company as well. I came up with the concept of a shared ownership and personal, professional, and financial (PPF) goal-planning organization. This moved the conversation from "who gets what" to a negotiation around how we can help each create value.

My thought was, instead of creating budgets that just included a line item for compensation, what if we also included a line item for compensating people through their personal, professional, and financial goals inside the business? It wasn't just wordplay or semantics—it was a real difference. In the new business model I envisioned, we wouldn't talk about the business owner's or franchisee's role in terms of hitting the targets *we* needed for us but rather setting targets they could accomplish for themselves and being smart enough at how to make the business work, because when the business wins, the owners win. These conversations focused on how the owners and their teams would hit their one-, three-, and five-year PPF goals. As long as the business owners and their teams did their part, they'd hit their goals and my new company would hit its goals as well.

Not every owner would have the same goals or would be willing to put the same effort into their business as others would. This new model would be flexible enough to allow us to devote only as many resources as were needed to help each owner achieve their goals, no matter what those goals were.

The company would have to be profitable enough to pay our management fee and co-share in our equity appreciation in order to qualify as a partner; those that weren't profitable enough would be taken on as customers, and once we grew them large enough, they then would qualify for the option to join us as partners. However, once we took them on as clients, our pathways to success would be aligned, not adversarial. What I envisioned and wanted to create was shared equity and decentralized organizational and ownership structure that allowed everyone to be empowered and aligned in creating value individually and collectively by working together.

Sonus had taught me that telling a business owner—one who had operated a business with *any* degree of success for decades—that I was going to buy them and deploy all sorts of new concepts, disciplines, and best practices, wouldn't work in the long term. Instead, I reasoned, it would be better to tell them how much I respected them and their company. Then I could explain to them the different businesses I'd built, including one engineered to help their business grow bigger, better, and faster and make more money and value not just for them but also for their peers who helped contribute IP and growth strategies. I would build additional group IP that they could individually and collectively share and deploy based on best practices, with everyone moving faster and having more impact together.

One of the biggest benefits I got from running Sonus was buying a business that was listed on a public stock exchange. This taught me the responsibility of looking at financials, having a system for governance, instilling discipline in the organization, and creating a process for how to make and implement decisions. Few business owners understood these skills, so transferring my knowledge to them was the germ of the idea that would become Audigy Group.

This was a fairly radical idea, so let me make an important point: when I criticized the conventional "B-School" thinking about the numbers never lying, I meant that the numbers weren't the point. The fact that a certain market can support projected revenues of XYZ may be as certain as gravity, but it does absolutely nothing to inspire people to go beyond their current level of belief or effectiveness or, dare I say, effort. Something else has to inspire them to think bigger and do more—to overcome the comfort with their income and help them see how much more they could aspire to and actually achieve.

My second epiphany occurred when I joined Hector's team at Primerica and witnessed an entirely new attitude in the workplace. At Primerica, most of the people I worked with showed great enthusiasm for learning and developing themselves. They devoted loads of energy to working extra hours and bringing in friends and showing them how to be successful. It looked like the polar opposite of traditional businesses where you put someone on payroll and they lived for the weekend. The energy at Primerica was intoxicating. Everyone wanted to test themselves to see how much they could grow.

Their motivation came less from what they did or what someone told them to do and more from their awareness that what they were doing could lead—would lead—to bigger opportunities. In traditional businesses, owners don't put much energy into painting a picture of growth for new talent. Primerica is set up to do exactly that by presenting a vivid picture of the ladder of upward mobility, a practice I would later develop into something I called an "employee maturity model." My employee maturity model shows you exactly what you can do to advance in an organization to reach your short-, medium-, and long-term goals. At Primerica, you have to obtain the right certifications to become an agent. You begin as an associate and as you sell more insurance and recruit more people to your team, you rise to senior associate, director, senior director, and so on. Primerica made it easy for people to show up and say, "Here's a picture of how I can become a million-dollar earner."

This is where Jim Collins's books *Good to Great*, *Great by Choice*, and *How the Mighty Fall* helped me understand how hierarchical structures, which are made up of people protecting their positions, tend to run off those who threaten their authority. Hierarchical structures tend to push good people away and institutionalize a certain complacent mindset. Even more harmfully, they discourage "intrapreneurship"—thinking like an entrepreneur from inside an organization. Many organizations ask their employees to "think like owners," which translates to sweating the details, being more accountable, working longer hours, and so on. But too often the concept doesn't extend to articulating anything concrete about rewarding these "owners" with professional and financial advancement.

When I thought about how to structure a career path for Audigy teammates, I didn't want to stop at vice president. I wanted my team to be able to know exactly how they could ascend through my organization until they blew through the C-Suite and became actual partners—with a small but tangible ownership of the company. At some point, I extended the notion of ownership to the idea of giving my client companies an equity stake in Audigy, thus closing the loop on incentivization, since their success would make them more valuable and their investment in Audigy more valuable.

I have heard people talk derisively about Primerica as a pyramid scheme, or tiered marketing and compensation scheme, as though the model was unethical (at worst) or irrelevant to traditional business models (at best). Primerica uses a tiered compensation model in which employees are incentivized not only to sell a product or service but also to recruit others to the company and to train them how to sell the company's products or services, after which they receive a percentage of each new hire's sales. The practice has gotten a bad name thanks to some shady characters in certain industries, but I think it has also received a bum rap.

Instead of resisting the idea of tiered compensation and marketing, I looked at the corporate structure at Primerica as one where everyone built his or her own business by creating a team of 3, of 30, of 300, or of 3,000 within their own business. It all depended on the hunger and leadership capacity of the individual.

In engineering Audigy, I would do the same thing. I would explain to every person who joined our team how to go from an entry-level position to being a future partner in the organization. And I would explain the pathway. In traditional business, people sign on to work for a salary, but nobody knows how to win in the big picture—i.e., how they can benefit and grow as the company benefits and grows. As a result, they revert to manipulation, games, and politics as the only weapons at their disposal to push back against the lack of clarity about opportunity. That Gallup poll cited earlier showing rampant disengagement among workers who actively sabotaged their place of work? Well, a business owner would do well to put in place a system that catered to the human appetite for success and gave their employees a clear understanding of how to pursue their own goals through pursuing the company's goals.

I realized that if I didn't show my star players what they could achieve, they would leave me. That would be a huge breaking point in my business, representing a loss of all the time I'd invested in training them. This was particularly relevant when a business reached the $25–$50 million range in revenues, at which point the most ambitious among your team come to feel the company has grown as large as it's going to grow. They may not realize that you intended to go to $100 million and, after that, on to $500 million. Because they don't see a future in which they can achieve their best professional, personal, and financial growth, they look for it somewhere else. And if they are any good, they usually find it.

But what if, instead of plodding through their resumes and treating them like human widgets, I asked prospective team members what their five-year and ten-year PPF targets were? Then I would ask, "What if I could show you how to accelerate your five-year target to year one? And what if I could show you how to accelerate your ten-year target to three years? Would you be willing to go all in and do whatever you need to do to develop into that position, no matter how hard it's going to be?"

Not everyone would be willing, but by breaking down the old ways of thinking about standards and expectations and time frames, I could attract the future rock stars. In such a model, not everyone would have to be a future partner in the making, either. Some might bring technical know-how but lack the business leadership orientation. All companies need these kinds of contributors, too, so that would be okay. But much like the Primerica model that rewards sales performance as well as team-building achievement, I would create compensation structures that rewarded team leaders for their own roles as leaders as well as their team's productivity.

■ ■ ■

When I ran my old company, Sonus, I had one hearing care provider in Chicago that was doing $1 million a year of personal production. All my other locations were averaging around $300,000 a year. Looking back, I realized the problem with this model of consolidation was that you had to raise capital to go out and find the deals, then take the time to close on the deals, acquire targets, close on them, and then integrate them into your business. But you couldn't operationalize the

acquired businesses fast enough to create a return on the capital out-
lays, so there was constant deficit financing. And because the owners
of the businesses couldn't see a bigger and clearer picture in which
they were going to win from doing things differently, they didn't put
in the effort to learn the newer, faster systems I made available to
them. It frustrated me to no end—but looking back, could I honestly
blame them?

But what if . . .

What if I had a consolidation company that already contained an
infrastructure with relatively little overhead, so that every business we
acquired was pure upside? Could this be done? I started going down
that rabbit hole and came up with the final draft of my new company.
The answer was to create a management company that provided rapid
operationalization of a business—all the nuts and bolts, from creating
a strategy in the first place to expertise in marketing, sales, operations,
people, finance, leadership, data, and technology—that allowed it to
focus on doing what it did best, which was working with its clients to
improve their hearing. To incentivize the businesses to believe in and
follow our lead, we would give them equity in our company.

I created a "reverse consolidation, decentralized ownership structure" LLC model registered in Washington State, because there you
can have up to three hundred business owners in different states and
with different names. In my traditional consolidation model, the kind
I built with Sonus, I would raise money, come in and buy your company, and cram my systems, operations, policies, procedures, budgets,
and expectations down on you. In my reverse consolidation model,
however, I would come in, give you equity in the management company, and effectively be your employee. I would work for you. If I was
successful, your business would grow; and the business we would be
partnered with, Audigy, would grow as well.

We would win together. And if it didn't work, I would carry
most of the risk. But I would need the client to trade off some

things in order to fund the project. For example, we would want the clients to buy their products and systems equipment through us so we could compete on costs in the industry. We'd take a management fee and also a little upside of their business in the form of equity. But their exit strategy would be simple: if it didn't work out, they could quit at any time. They just couldn't leave with any equity in Audigy beyond what had already been paid out in the form of dividends, effectively forfeiting their equity in the management company if they quit. But, I promised, if they stayed and we ever sold the business, they would be a shareholder with me and they would get the benefit of the sale.

Thinking differently can challenge, and even scare, most people, so I had to draw clients in by emphasizing that the whole point of reverse consolidation was to make it easier for them to be successful.

Here, I could draw on my experience at Primerica as an example. While I was dreaming up Audigy, I became fascinated by the Primerica model and decided to try it. I got my life insurance and securities license, which are required to sell Primerica's products, then one day I walked up to my friend and said, "Hey, Hector. I just got my life insurance and securities license. Can I sign up on your team?"

Hector started laughing. "You're going to go out and do kitchen table appointments?" he asked.

"Yeah, dude, that's exactly what I'm going to do," I told him. "You told me how you went from zero to a million, and I need to experience it myself or I won't be able to teach it to other people."

Hector was intrigued and impressed that I was humble enough to want to get close to him and learn from him by doing it. After all, I had just come from a position as the CEO of a public company. So I became a Primerica associate and ended up recruiting half a dozen people right off the bat and teaching them. Applying the principles and techniques I learned from recording Hector and from my readings, I began to build a nice little business inside Primerica. When

I was an associate there, I was able to log into my portal each day. I had every document and every training tool I needed right at my fingertips. I used the portal to transact business, invoice clients, collect payments, and receive my checks from Primerica each month. Primerica made it very easy for me to focus on doing the thing that directly contributed to my success, which was getting in front of people.

I wanted to create the same kind of optimized, high-performance engine at Audigy. If successful, I could change the way small businesses were run. My challenge would be to convince mom-and-pop owners, many of whom viewed themselves as capable business people who had made good lives for themselves and their families, to let me show them how to run their business better and to do the work of training their team, managing their money, and building their infrastructure out beyond anything they could do alone. While a management fee was indispensable for my business to operate effectively, I didn't think it would pose a hurdle for owners because it was less expensive to tap into my variable-expense structure—you pay for what you need and use—than to use the fixed-expense structure of hiring and training and offering benefits to dozens of new employees.

And if you didn't like doing business with us, it would be just as if you'd made any bad hire: you were perfectly free to fire us. But if you liked the arrangement and began to see how it allowed you to be more successful, to have a better quality of life, and to own a piece of Audigy along with me, what did you have to lose?

▪ ▪ ▪

When my noncompete with Sonus expired, I was eager to move forward. My plan was to keep my team in place at Primerica and continue to draw income there, but when I registered Audigy, the Securities and Exchange Commission rejected my request since I had obtained my license to sell securities through Primerica. Legally, I could only sell securities through them. Both Hector and I could get into a lot of trouble with the SEC if I tried to wiggle around this rule. So when I was ready to start Audigy, the members of my Primerica team and their accounts were handed over to Hector to enjoy the fruits of our labor.

Well, almost all of them. There were a few promising folks I brought along with me to Audigy as my first employees.

For additional resources, get immediate access to exclusive behind the scenes videos that uncover even more items I couldn't share in this book. To access these exclusive resources, visit NineFigureTools.com

CHAPTER 6

Why Settle for Realistic?

When I ran Sonus, I rarely had much to do with hiring. I focused on buying businesses, raising capital, and doing the systems development and systems building side of the business. My human resources staff handled recruiting. That choice didn't always serve us well, because traditional HR methods often don't grasp the idiosyncrasies that can make people rock stars or duds. In building Audigy, I was determined to learn how to prospect people, since I would be building the business from scratch.

I began learning how to do this at Primerica, which rewarded associates both for their own performance and the performances of those whom they recruited to their teams and trained to become associates like themselves. Armed with new knowledge and confidence from my mentorship with Hector, I learned how to recruit people using my own idiosyncratic methods. For example, rather than run classified ads or work through recruitment agencies, I looked for engaging and quick-thinking people in other places like grocery stores, barbershops, and car dealerships. I'd try to engage them in conversations about their careers and let them know I was starting a company that was looking for extraordinary people.

One day, on the way to pick up my daughter from school, I stopped by the Ferrari dealership with the idea of spending half an hour doing a little prospecting for potential employees/associates/team members for Primerica. As soon as I walked into the showroom, a young man jumped out of a chair and walked over and started talking to me. He told me he was studying business at the University of Portland and working at the dealership part-time. He did a great job engaging me with his bright personality.

At some point, I said something like, "Well, I'm not going to buy anything today, thanks and good luck," and started to leave.

That's when he said, "Hey, you gotta see something. You've probably never seen it, and you're never going to buy it. I would never buy it because they're not supposed to be very reliable, but you have to see it!"

The man, whose name was Mason Walker, took me into the garage, and there stood an absolutely, ridiculously badass Jaguar XK-100 someone had traded in for a Ferrari.

"The only way I can drive it is if I'm with a client," Mason explained. "I want to drive this car. Will you take ten minutes and go for a quick drive with me?"

I said sure, and we jumped into the Jag. This guy was so good, I thought. He drove, then I drove, and I asked him to fast-forward and tell me what he planned to do when he graduated from college.

"What is your dream?" I asked.

"I would like to sell enough cars that one day the owner puts *me* in charge of running this Ferrari dealership," he told me.

"That's so sad," I replied.

Taken aback, Mason asked me why I thought making half a million dollars a year, being able to attend all of Ferrari's events, owning a Ferrari, and doing what he'd always dreamed of was sad.

"Can I ask you a question?" I countered.

"Sure."

"What if someone could teach you how to eventually own your own Ferrari dealership? Would you want to learn from this person?" I asked.

"Sure . . ." he responded tentatively.

"Then come see me Tuesday night, and I'll get you started learning how to dream bigger than you thought you had any right to." And then I explained to him all about Primerica. Of the hundred people I'd invited to the presentation, around twenty showed up, including Mason. And of those twenty, Mason showed the most promise and was the most eager to learn. A bit later, I told him about my plan to launch Audigy. We talked a little about the concept, and I asked him to think about his financial goals. He said that being worth $10 million could change his life.

"I didn't know what to base that on," Mason said in a podcast we did together years later. "But it sounded like a lot."

Then I popped the question.

"How would you like to be my first employee? I'll promise you that if you do everything I tell you to and stick with me until we sell the business, you'll make that $10 million."

And that's how I convinced a man who dreamed of working his way up the ranks of a car dealership to take a risk with someone he didn't know all that well. But the trust was there. That's when something extraordinary happened.

■ ■ ■

Three years before my joyride with Mason, I was living in Portland and running Sonus. One of my best friends at the time was Larry Meyers. Larry had run a division of my stepdad's company. During my stepdad and mom's divorce, Larry came over to Sonus to work as my chief operating officer. In Larry, I found someone who I grew to admire and respect and trust. Although he chose to continue to live in

Dallas, Larry rented an apartment in Portland. I counted him among my cigar and martini buddies—which are the very best kind—and we loved sitting by a fire and talking about our business and my crazy family goings-on.

One day after dinner at a restaurant, Larry, a Vietnam veteran, complained of not feeling well. I chalked it up to a bout of food poisoning, but it turned out to be something far different and worse. He was diagnosed with lung cancer, brought on by wartime exposure to Agent Orange. He underwent surgery but only lived a short while longer. I cleaned out his apartment and put everything in storage. It was a deeply sad time for all of us who knew Larry.

Here's the punch line to Larry's story: Several years later, Mason was in the process of moving out of his dorm and finding an apartment to rent in Portland. Like most college graduates, Mason had minimal furniture, so we took a trip to my storage unit where Larry's stuff was being kept and outfitted him pretty well for a recent grad. I helped him and his buddies load up a U-Haul trailer with all of Larry's old apartment furniture and drive it to Mason's new place. I had no idea where exactly Mason was moving, so I was flabbergasted when we pulled up in front of the same apartment building where Larry had lived.

We got on to the elevator and Mason hit the button for the fifth floor. I gasped. Everyone looked at me.

"What's the matter?" said Mason.

"This was Larry's floor," I said, and told them about my best friend. "He was at the end of this hallway, on the left."

Now, it was Mason's turn to gasp.

"No way! That's the apartment I rented."

"I cannot freaking believe this," I said, although not exactly in those words.

I told the guys more about Larry. I am a person of faith who believes the world sends you all sorts of messages if you're paying attention.

After Mason moved in, I went over for supper one night and the two of us just sat there for a few moments, thinking the same thing. Mason's ending up here was Larry's idea, and we could feel him saying, "You two are just gonna kill it!"

Mason had chosen to work at the Ferrari dealership not only to earn money but also to expand his network.

"I thought, what better way of doing that than being able to be at the Ferrari and Maserati dealership?" he told me. "Anyone who spent a quarter of a million dollars on a discretionary product like a car was someone I wanted to know and who I wanted to know me."

What he did not know was that he was going to run into someone who wasn't just there for a transaction and didn't look at him as just a salesguy. I was the first one to engage with him and find out where he was in his life and in his thinking. I was the first one to ask him questions that made him rethink some of his assumptions and put him in an uncomfortable position to see how he handled himself and whether he could change his mind in the face of a compelling argument. Most important, Mason recalled, "That's the first time someone challenged me on whether *good enough* really was good. When you think about what's possible, why settle for what's realistic?"

His was the kind of thinking I needed employees to understand so that Audigy would be successful; my team would need to be on the same page with our thinking. To bring on my first employee, there was still one missing piece of the puzzle: the matter of Mason's salary. I offered him $41,000, which was less than half what he had been earning part-time at the dealership while going to school.

"I was on the sidewalk in downtown Portland, and I just kind of stopped and thought to myself, 'What an insult!'" recalled Mason. He pushed back, so I laid out the situation as clearly as I could.

"Let me ask you this one question, and before you answer this question, I want you to think about it. Because the answer that you provide is going to determine whether you pursue net worth or you pursue income."

I asked Mason how he expected me to invest in him if he was unwilling to invest in himself. Investing in himself didn't mean leasing a BMW and renting an upscale condo; it meant driving an old Dodge pickup and living in a less expensive place for a while.

"This is how you earn your equity. This is how you seize your opportunity. Remember," I emphasized, "I'm not looking for an employee; I'm looking for a business partner. I'm looking for someone who sees through 'the sure thing' because the sure thing is only sure until whoever it was who hired you doesn't need you anymore."

I'd experienced that in my life in one form or another; I don't know whether Mason's youth had shielded him from that cruel reality thus far, but I assured him that was not the way we were going to build Audigy. And that, in a nutshell, was the pitch I would use not only to recruit gifted people like Mason and others who would join us, but also the clients who might be wondering whether their businesses could offer them more.

■ ■ ■

In the early days of Audigy, we scoured our contact lists and sent mailers to everyone we could think of. We kicked off the business June 16, 2005, at the Phoenician Hotel in Scottsdale, Arizona, with eighteen businesses that had signed on for my recruitment presentation. Unlike Sonus, Audigy didn't require gobs of money to start—just $120,000, which represented three months of operating capital. Our target going into the sales presentations, which I called "guest summits," was to generate $22,000 in future business, which bought us two more weeks of existence. This amount also took into account a cash reserve fund I would build to take care of future growth needs, including my salary.

When I got my commission report a month later, it turned out we'd generated $76,000 in revenue instead of the targeted $22,000.

"It looks like we've bought ourselves a month and half of staying in business!" I told my team. But I put the extra money we made into the cash reserves rather than go out and blow it on something. In the coming years, this fiscal prudence would be a best practice that I would teach thousands of businesspeople; it was something I had been doing for years.

Our goal was to generate enough funds for the first two weeks, a month's worth, and then to acquire ninety days of revenue so there would be enough in the bank for three months of operating expenses if revenues suddenly dried up. It continued for thirty-six months until, one day, my comptroller came in and said, "Hey, Brandon. We have a new problem."

"Yeah? What's our new problem?"

"We have $5.8 million in cash reserves and we're only spending a fraction of that, so we've basically got fifteen months of cash in the bank," said the comptroller.

We went to a bank for counseling on how to ladder our cash by investing in bonds with differing maturity, so that the money could work for us while remaining available as we needed it. But we had proven the algorithm for how to build a successful business without needing outside investment. This was a huge lesson for me that I would pass along to my clients: many businesses fail due to lack of demand for their product or service, the inability to hire talented people to their team, and the lack of financing. They are related. If you don't have a great product or service, talented people aren't going to want to hitch their wagon to your vision, and certainly no one is going to give you money. And if you can't present a clear growth trajectory to your people, they won't be able to see how they can grow personally, professionally, and financially with your business. The prospect of someday getting financing may attract some to your concept, but there is a lot of downside risk to this decision as well, which may deter them.

Using cash flow as a strategy for start-up growth puts your success in your own hands, along with your willingness to do whatever it takes to achieve your dream. This was the message I delivered in those first years at Audigy as growing numbers of mom-and-pop businesses in the hearing care industry began attending my guest summits. ·

Each of the guest summits went more or less like this: The lights would come down. I would walk to the front of the room. And I would turn a projector on with slides illustrating the concepts from books like *Cashflow Quadrant*, and I would start talking. The themes were easy to create because they were rooted in the readings I'd done and the lessons I'd learned by videotaping and spending time with Hector. They also followed the same logic I applied to my own creation of Audigy.

"If you had the choice of building your business bigger, better, faster, more profitable, and in such a way that you could differentiate yourself from the rest of the marketplace, would you want to do it?" I asked them.

"Of course," "Why, yes," and "Sure," would emanate from around the room.

Many of those who came to the presentations knew me from Sonus, so I enjoyed telling them that Audigy was the opposite of Sonus in that it would be owned by its members. No one else had ever done anything like it, not only in our industry, but in any industry that I was aware of. When you launch a business, it's very important to know exactly to whom you're directing your message. In our case, we were not trying to win business from the prospective entrepreneur. Our audiences were small businesses that were already enjoying a measure of success. The owners were making a good living, good enough to put roofs over their heads, feed their families, and finance vacations and college educations. Most were well educated—more formally than me, at any rate—and many had advanced medical degrees.

But, in one way or another, they felt stuck. That was what had made them pull the trigger and pay a few thousand bucks to come hear my presentation. Maybe the problem was that they needed to hire new people but didn't know how to source talent or develop it from within. Or perhaps they were feeling pressure from new competitors in their area and didn't know how to fight back and dominate their marketplace. In most cases, problems boiled down to the fact that the business owners had strong technical knowledge of their field and solid work ethics, but they lacked leadership skills and, in many cases, the business systems and planning skills needed to grow beyond a few million in revenue a year.

Still, we had our work cut out for us in changing the business owners' thinking from conventional terms to Audigy's terms. This involved changing their mindsets twice.

First, they needed to check conventional wisdom at the door, snap out of years of comfortable emotional investment in themselves as experts, and realize that they needed business help. They were pros in understanding hearing, and I wasn't going to improve upon their expertise, but I sure as shootin' could help them run a better business. However, in order for me to help them, they had to embrace curiosity and experimentation.

To provide context to my audiences, I gave them an overview of the very real industry pressures on the mom-and-pop business, especially the consolidation of power in fewer and fewer manufacturers that were essentially buying customers to sell to. This is what Starkey eventually did, and also what Sonus did on behalf of other manufacturing partners.

Given the nature of this consolidation, plus the rise of new Bluetooth technologies and an emerging direct-to-consumer market for multifunctional sound systems that included hearing aids, I painted a compelling picture for why it would be wise for these owners to have Audigy in their corner.

Second, I explained that there was a type of business ownership to which they could aspire that differed from their current model. As we've already covered here, one of the common errors among small business owners is a tendency to wear too many hats and effectively do everyone else's job. Most business owners, including me, have been guilty of this at some time or another in their careers. But this kind of business ownership is more akin to freelance work, in which you "own" your job but have to do all, or much, of the work yourself. Thanks to Hector and others, my definition of business ownership evolved to where I viewed it as having other people doing the work for you so you can guide the strategic growth and direction of the organization. Truth be told, I had discovered the beauty of this model myself all those years ago when I "hired" the senior class at my high school to harvest my family's walnut orchard!

This strategic mindset and the leadership skills required to inspire others to help you implement your strategy were precisely the qualities my clients lacked and precisely those Audigy could provide. This would open up entirely new and larger vistas of personal, professional, and financial growth than these quondam experts could have imagined.

▪ ▪ ▪

Audigy began as something of a family company, albeit not one family but several. In addition to Mason, his sister started interning with us and eventually ran our marketing department. My dad started working with us as well, so I guess in one respect we were a pop-and-son business. Mason was a conduit to many talented people who came to work for us. Some of the programs that the original group put into place proved staples of the organization until we sold it.

But we had a hard environment, as well—one in which I could be a tough coach. Once, Mason's sister told me she wasn't in Audigy to make money like her brother.

"I'm just here to have a great job," she said.

I asked her to leave my office and think about what she had said. When she asked why, I told her that until she respected the fact that she should be paid for her contributions to the organization, I could not fully believe in her. She left and returned an hour later, ready to talk about her salary from the point of view of someone who deserved to make a lot of money because of the value she brought to the organization. When we sold the business, the money she got was life-changing for her, so being tough during a teachable moment proved the right course to take.

When I told the business owners who had taken time out of their week to come listen to me, "Hey, listen up. You need to disengage from the day-to-day stuff and be coaching and mentoring your team to do it so you can plan," I had only to look to my own team for inspiration. When Mason came to work for me, he sold his BMW and got rid of his fancy apartment—the one Larry used to live in—to drive my old pickup and live in a rental house we used to own. When he asked me for a promotion early on in our collaboration, I recommended that he work on being recognized as a leader by his peers rather than rely on being elevated by me.

"My job isn't to promote you," I argued. "Your job is to make it impossible not to be promoted."

And in 2006, when he floated the topic of a raise by me, I suggested he "go and earn your raise" by hitting his end-of-year target for recruiting new members to his team.

Sound like a hard-ass, don't I? Well, yes.

For the final quarter of 2006, I wanted us to have our biggest event ever at Caesar's Palace in Las Vegas. One of the target groups we invited to the event included doctors who were considering opening audiology practices. Typically, we brought in twenty or twenty-five such guests to an audiology practice development seminar. For this grand finale in 2006, I wanted to double that figure. Mason and his team worked their butts off and met their target of fifty new members. Having worked so hard for this success, everyone in the company was jazzed and loving life, which is the way you feel when you've set an aggressive target and met it.

I had such faith that Mason and his team would be successful that, unbeknownst to him, I had done a little advance planning on a special bonus for him once the event was over. Here's how it went down. I recalled a conversation about cars we'd had years earlier. We're both serious car aficionados, and I asked him if he could have bought any new car, what would it be?

"A loaded silver BMW 550 with black interior," Mason had replied without missing a beat.

I never forgot that conversation.

Just after the Las Vegas event, I asked Mason what he had going on for lunch. He said he was free. I told him I needed to meet with an accountant on the other side of town. Did Mason want to come and join me? After the meeting, we could go out and have lunch and celebrate the amazing event that we just had. We got into my car and drove across town to the accountant's office, which turned out to be closed. It didn't matter because I had no appointment scheduled, anyway, but Mason didn't know that. So, I suggested we kill time and check out the new cars and kick some tires at a BMW dealership across the street from the accountant's office until the accountant showed up for the (nonexistent) meeting.

On the way to the dealership, I reminded Mason about that conversation. He remembered it clearly. After arriving at the dealership, we walked into the showroom and Mason stopped in his tracks. There, gleaming in silver with a black interior, was a BMW 550 packed with every option under the sun, including a full body kit. As Mason gaped at the car, I said, "That's a beauty. Let's check it out."

Mason walked around the car to check out the pricing and spec sheet, which was posted on a Plexiglas stand beside the vehicle. Instead of the specs, there was a note on dealership letterhead reading, "Congratulations, Mason Walker, for reaching all your goals. Love, Brandon."

I gave him the rest of the day off to enjoy his well-earned bonus.

For additional resources, get immediate access to exclusive behind the scenes videos that uncover even more items I couldn't share in this book. To access these exclusive resources, visit NineFigureTools.com

CHAPTER 7

Audigy Group Is a Success

One of the most important qualities you need to succeed as an entrepreneur is self-awareness. Of course, I didn't know this until I learned it from Hector and the other great business thinkers I met and whose books I read during my sabbatical. What I learned about myself was that I am an energetic, hard-driving person who feels comfortable with risk and with diving into new opportunities and figuring out what to do as I go along.

The benefit of being wired this way is that I try new opportunities others might overlook or shy away from and, once I commit to a course of action, pursue them until I succeed. But my personality type does have a drawback or two, which includes impatience with others who don't seem to get things as quickly as I do or who lack my level of confidence in bold action. In the past, I viewed those deficits with impatience and dismissed people who exhibited them as inadequate. But I'd come to appreciate different kinds of personal work styles and decision-making time frames in others since creating Audigy.

In building Audigy, I quickly learned to ditch the bull-in-the-china-shop approach to influencing other people to follow me. For example, I knew that persuading the owners of audiology clinics to become members of Audigy was only half (or maybe two-thirds) of the battle. Yes, I had to educate them about the challenges they faced in their marketplaces and offer a convincing case that their best bet to compete was to ally with me. For example, the very first founder I had at Audigy was Dr. Izzy Kirsch. Izzy had a very large practice in New Jersey, and when I showed him what I wanted to do, he immediately said, "I have to do this with you, and we can change the face of private practice."

In the case of Izzy, he was founder number one and when we sold the business, he was still my partner and made more money in the sale of Audigy than his business was doing in revenue when he first joined me. Having the opportunity to start something with someone who shares such a significant vision is something I will always cherish.

It often happened with owners, and Izzy was no exception, that had to go back to their businesses and convince their team of the same thing of which I'd just convinced them. Translating what they heard from me to their employees proved difficult for many owners, so I arranged for meetings with their staff.

One such company was owned by the Wilkins family who attended one of our events at Caesar's Palace in 2006. One of the co-owners, Jeff, told me that he and his brother, Matt, were in "a weird spot" because they and their father ran the company as equal partners even though the sons were more ambitious about growth. They were making about $3 million a year in revenue and seemed unable, or unwilling, to take the next steps to grow their business. I had the feeling part of the issue stemmed from the fact that their father was approaching retirement age and wanted to wind down rather than ramp up. Anyway, two years went by and I heard from Jeff, who wanted to talk about joining Audigy.

Two developments prompted Jeff and Matt to reconnect with me. First, their father had retired, and Jeff and Matt wanted to pull out the stops on growing their company. Second, they had gone ahead and opened a few more offices, only to discover they were unable to get their arms around managing and growing their business.

"We are fairly successful in making money," Jeff told me during a meeting. "But there are a lot of processes we don't have in place and, to tell you the truth, there were too many moving parts for us to juggle. We're feeling stuck. Let's talk about how you might help us and what we can do to grow the company."

Jeff and I talked about the challenges to joining Audigy. Chief among them was allowing a third party into their business. Change is never an easy thing and it can be harder when you have to turn some degree of control over to someone else and do things a little differently—especially when it involves somebody who hasn't grown up with your business.

"At some point," I told Jeff, "you're going to have to stand in front of your audiologist or your employees and say, 'Look, we're bringing this guy on because he's got some great ideas. We want to see growth for everyone in the business, but we're going to have to learn a new system and it's a little scary, I understand."

The biggest challenge for all small business owners involved the selling process. I had developed a booklet called *Patients for Life* (PFL), which outlined an approach to hearing care that guided patients step-by-step through the process of hearing loss and how people experience it in their daily lives. The booklet also provided my professional people with a blueprint for engaging patients in making bigger investments in their hearing than they were used to. The process focused more on persistence over time—not just matching a hearing test score with a device, but building in upgrade plans to leverage new technologies and respond to the progression of hearing loss.

The "patients for life" approach required greater scripting on the part of the professional team, who pushed back because they thought it was unnecessarily complicated. At first, neither Jeff or Matt liked the feel of the new script either. But once they got in front of their patients and began to use it, they discovered that they and their patients understood hearing loss better than they ever had before. Suddenly, Jeff's salespeople began saying, "You know, this guy Dawson knows what he's doing."

To cement the learning for Jeff and Matt's team, I came in and did some role-playing, a practice I still use today in training. Sometimes I played the patient; other times I stepped in as a professional, and the professional person would play the patient. This enabled the employees to see the patient-employee dynamic at work in a safe but realistic setting. The staff got to see how every point of confusion or reluctance expressed by a patient could be turned into an opportunity to solve a problem.

For example, say a customer asked one of our professional people why they should buy our hearing aids when they were being sold cheaper down the street. After complimenting the customer on their question, the professional would lead them through a series of questions to engage them in the process of discovery. Were they aware of the difference between cutting-edge technologies like ours and older technologies that only call themselves that? After all, you have to compare apples with apples, right? Were they aware that a strong majority of people were disappointed with their buying decision? This gave our professional people the opportunity to educate the customer about the different levels of investment they could make in hearing aid technology depending on what mattered most to them—how it integrated into their lifestyle.

Needless to say, few, if any, competitors took the time to educate prospective customers to this extent, a fact that allowed us to ask the customer what their level of confidence would be in a hearing aid seller who wasn't going to take the time to understand what was important to them. Their level of confidence was usually pretty low, and it sank even lower when we mentioned the Audigy certificate of guarantee, which said that if for any reason you were disappointed in your purchase decision or we did not integrate it into your life within ninety days, you would get all your money back.

As a result of our patient, methodical approach to working with Jeff's team, his staff's reluctance toward Audigy quickly waned after they had the opportunity to see us in action. Not long after Jeff and Matt's dad retired, Jeff brought me into a company meeting and told the staff that we'd be working more closely together from then on. Jeff particularly depended on us for training new staff, which was an important part of growing a business that many smaller companies outsourced to vendors who supplied cookie-cutter methods, or tried to do in-house using senior staff who may have been good at their jobs but didn't know how to train people. They signed on with us in 2008 and sold their company in 2017, at which point their revenues were at $14 million, triple what they'd been before working with us.

"After all the coaching you did with me and my leadership team and all the training you did with my employees, probably the smartest thing we learned from you was how to exit—first from day-to-day overseeing of the business and then actually selling it," Jeffrey once told me. "We learned how to let the business start growing by itself through our team so that when we went to sell the business, we weren't required to be with the business." It felt unbelievably rewarding to be able to help that family get their business to a point where they were able to sell it for one of the highest prices ever received in the industry.

One of my most loyal clients is Dr. Mary Lou Luebbe, the president of Luebbe Hearing Services. We met back when I was growing up and working at Starkey for my stepdad and mom (she bought hearing aids from Starkey), so we went way back!

When I began working with Luebbe Hearing Services, the company was already well established in the industry. Mary Lou's father had started it in 1946 to help World War II veterans who were returning from battle with hearing loss. Mary Lou had become a member at

Sonus while I was there, strictly for the buying advantages of belong-ing to a network of similar businesses. By the time I emerged from my sabbatical after leaving Sonus, Mary Lou was also feeling the itch for something more. She didn't want to change careers—she was born into hearing care services and remains passionately devoted to the field.

We had stayed in touch, and when I started Audigy, I recruited her hard. After some deliberation, she sent me a fax: a picture of a dozen eggs, sitting in a basket. Mary Lou put all her eggs with Aud-igy. She's continued to work with me since 2006, and today her busi-ness has three offices in Ohio.

Mary Lou was a classic Audigy client in the best sense: she loved her profession and serving people and was technically accomplished as an audiologist. However, she lacked some of the basic business skills—such as planning, assessment, leadership and employee devel-opment, and goal-setting—that characterize successful business lead-ers. The Brandon who emerged from his sabbatical was a different creature than the one she'd known at Starkey and Sonus. It was no longer all about *him*; now it was about *we*, and what *she* could accom-plish by collaborating with Audigy to help more people enjoy healthy hearing than she'd ever thought possible.

Mary Lou prefers not to use specific numbers, but she was also a classic Audigy success story in that she increased her revenues and profitability severalfold in a shorter period of time than we'd planned, and did so without relinquishing her youthful enthusiasm for making a difference in her clients' lives. For my team, part of the reward of working with Mary Lou was helping her discover pockets of potential excellence in her small team of half a dozen or so, while weeding out a couple of players she felt had never really committed to the company.

"I think things happen for a reason," Mary Lou told me once. "I believe that you make your own good luck, or bad luck as the case might be. And it has a lot to do with the people that you associate with."

▪ ▪ ▪

To ensure that our clients were associating with the best people in the business at Audigy, I implemented something I called an Employee Maturity Model, which provided the framework for my teams to develop themselves, with my help, and to advance in the organization. Because no two people had the same ambition, talent, capacity, or goals, the model allowed for individual development in line with each team member's goals and Audigy's goals. Unlike most leadership development programs, my model didn't have a set advancement structure etched in stone (e.g., spend *this* much time accomplishing certain things and you will advance to *that*). Instead, it rewarded actual maturation and leadership developed in the course of learning and contributing to the organization. You didn't get a promotion and then begin doing new things and having new responsibilities; on the contrary—it was only after you began to mature, think for yourself, take on new challenges, and improve something at Audigy that you were recognized with a new title and salary.

My first employee, Mason, offered a case in point. He had eight different bosses before he became the president and then CEO of Audigy. Even though he and I enjoyed the special bond that comes from starting out together at ground zero, he soon got a serious dose of business realism as we brought on more experienced and senior people who had certain competencies we needed to help the company grow.

I knew it was hard for someone who had given his blood, sweat, and tears working side by side with me to bring Audigy to life to have to watch one big shot after another swoop into the company and take a job he likely thought he should have had. But he wasn't ready, a fact I reminded him of regularly—along with a promise, of sorts.

One day, Mason came into my office and asked to speak with me for a moment. I could tell not all was right with him—he had a conflicted look in his eye.

"I'm really not aligning with that new guy I'm reporting to," he confided to me. "He wants to do things the way he knows how, and isn't listening to my ideas."

Mason confessed that he had even mulled over quitting.

My reply might have been to ask him the nature of the disagreement, but doing so would have ignored the lesson in maturity that was staring Mason in the eye. So, instead of giving him the shoulder he wanted to cry on or the authority he lacked to push back against his boss, I said, "Look, Mason. You could throw in the towel, but what's that going to teach you? That giving up is great? You're going to have lots of bosses. That's a given. What's not a given is what you learn from them." I went on to say that there was plenty he could learn from people he didn't particularly get along with. For one, he could develop technical competencies he didn't have. For another, he could learn what not to do or how not to behave when *he* became boss someday.

"As long as you always perform at the highest level culturally and operationally by learning, you'll ascend above your bosses," I told Mason. "Remember, when I hired you, I wanted a partner, not an employee. But that takes time." In 2011, I promoted him to president of the company; in addition, when we sold he made over $10 million in the sale and today he is the CEO.

▪ ▪ ▪

During my sabbatical, I read that consulting companies that generated $250,000 of revenue per employee usually cleared a profit of around 20 percent. With this figure stuck in the back of my head, I went back and reverse engineered my seven years of running Sonus to determine what kind of profit margins I had achieved. The most profitable year was the last one, when I was looking at around $72 million in revenues, but I discovered it took me seven years to hit $250,000 in revenues per employee, which is why I lost money for the first six years. I had 260 or so employees, so my profits had been much smaller than 20 percent. I decided that when I started Audigy, I was going to use the $250,000 of revenue per employee as my low-end baseline for growing the company. I would never dip below this level of productivity, but I would certainly strive to beat it.

I scaled Audigy according to that algorithm until I got it up to $325,000–$350,000 per employee. I spoke to some friends in private equity who told me about companies that were doing as much as $500,000 per employee, though they were typically technology companies. To this day, I teach business owners who attend our workshops on building businesses about this rule. It's a perfect example of one of those metrics that business owners don't know they don't know, and from the beginning they proved it time and time again in the workshops. I'd ask a participant how much the company made. They'd say $3 million. I'd ask how many employees they had. They'd tell me thirty. I'd tell them they had what I called a "thin and wide" business that, like a spaghetti noodle, would break and fail as they got bigger.

Of course, they would beg to differ. So I'd find someone else in the group who was making $3 million with a team of twelve rather than thirty. And we'd account for the different industries, if they were different, and explore why one business operated profitably with fewer than half the employees of the other. The lesson, I would suggest again, is that the biggest threat to a growing business are the things we don't know we don't know. These things could be psychological, such as lacking the confidence to expect more from yourself and your employees. Or they could be financial, such as not fully appreciating what makes a business profitable.

Overall, businesses were incredibly enthusiastic about joining Audigy. The greatest resistance we felt stemmed from the business owners' allegiance to their suppliers. As a former Starkey employee and consolidator at Sonus, I recognized these allegiances for exactly what they were. The clinics wanted the cheapest possible price and a steady product, and the manufacturers wanted guaranteed customers.

At Sonus, I ran interference between the clinics and manufacturers by offering a private label Sonus hearing package, three years of replacement batteries, three years of loss and damage coverage, marketing collateral support, and a limited amount of management support the clinics were free to follow or not. Most did not.

At Audigy, I offered all those replacement guarantees but also far, far deeper engagement in their businesses. First, rather than ask members to simply accept whatever devices manufacturers made, we were going to design our own devices to meet their patients' needs.

"Do you want to be a consumer of someone else's innovations or innovate on your own terms?" I asked. "Do you want to work with a supplier we can actually direct in the product they build for us?" I got together with my buddy, Mike Mann, who was in charge of global manufacturing for Siemens Healthcare, and we created a product roadmap of every single feature set in the industry. Then I put it in front of the Audigy clients and showed them what they could have with Audigy. Believe it or not, that was the hook.

From 2008 to 2012, when the world went into recession, Audigy grew by leaps and bounds. We received awards for six straight years from the *Oregon Business Journal* as the number one fastest-growing private company on the West Coast, and won five *Inc. Magazine* 500 awards, three top workplace awards, two entrepreneur-of-the-year awards for me, and many other accolades. When we sold the company in 2016, we had 198 employees who worked as members of strategic business units for our 280 business owners. Each of them was three-and-a-half to fifteen times larger than anyone else in the industry. We sold Audigy for strategic reasons as the industry began contracting, with fewer and fewer manufacturers retooling to compete directly against our clients. If they couldn't get products by agreeing to work with a supplier, they were out of business. The company still exists, with Mason—hired off the lot of a car dealership—as its leader. Audigy thrives in its marketplace, and those who stayed earned millions from the sale.

At this point, I was ready to devote the next year to a second sabbatical. Some aspects of the sabbatical would be similar to the first—reading lots of books and networking with lots of people who had something to teach me. But other parts of it would be intentionally different this time around because this time it wouldn't be just me transitioning to a new phase of my journey. This time I'd be joined by a remarkable woman named Natalie Workman, and it wouldn't be just me adding to my legacy but rather the two of us building a legacy of helping others realize their dreams.

For additional resources, get immediate access to exclusive behind the scenes videos that uncover even more items I couldn't share in this book. To access these exclusive resources, visit NineFigureTools.com

CHAPTER 8

Work and Marriage

According to the US Census Bureau, there were around 7.9 million business establishments operated by couples in 2022, employing 131 million people. Over half—3.76 million businesses— had five or fewer employees, for a total of almost 6 million workers (including owners). Many of the owners I worked with at Sonus and later at Audigy fell into the mom-and-pop category. While this may conjure up a quaint image of couples working contentedly side-by-side, such businesses are anything but quaint. A better description might be "fraught," or "challenging."

A marriage is like a business partnership: when you are in a bad partnership, everything around you suffers because you can only focus on what's wrong. But partnership in marriage is more important than partnership in business, especially when children are involved, so I believe married couples should do everything in their power to realign when things go wrong. But if realignment is impossible and both of you can see you're going to spend the rest of your life working against each other rather than for each other, you have to end the partnership for the good of everyone.

As I organized my lessons about running a business into a coherent program to help other entrepreneurs avoid some of the problems

I had faced, I also reflected on the challenges I'd faced in my marriages. Prior to marrying Natalie, I was married and divorced twice. As you'll see, balancing family and business life for an entrepreneur is not unrelated. My first wife, Tracy, and I married in 1990 when we were in our early twenties. She was, and is, a sweet and wonderful woman with whom I am still friends. Her dream in life was to live on a farm like the one her parents owned, a beautiful thousand-acre dairy farm that had cows and dogs all over the place. She wanted to stay as far away from corporate America as she could. You might say we were both after a version of the American Dream, but my version was far too risky and, even if successful, a far cry from her vision of rural bliss.

It didn't take very long for us to realize we wanted totally different kinds of lives. We began to feel so awkwardly incompatible that we used to laugh about our incompatibility. Humor is a far better emotion to fall back on than spite and resentment, but even humor can't save a marriage between two people with radically opposed visions of the good life. Even though we had two young daughters, Brianna and Samantha, we divorced amicably in 2001.

I met my second wife, Tammy, at the beginning of 2001. She was an interior designer for Nike. We married in May 2004 and were together for thirteen years. Although she worked, she stayed close to home to take care of our daughter, Ciara, as well as my daughters from my first marriage, who lived with us on and off all through their high school years. For the first eleven years of our marriage, I traveled more and more and showed no sign of slowing down. After I turned forty-two and Audigy became successful, Tammy would constantly remind me that when I turned forty-five, she expected me to retire and reminded me that if that did not prove to be the case, we wouldn't make it. She wanted me to be home more and to pour myself into our family life full-time. I would try to brush off her comments with little attempts at quips, but by the time I turned forty-five, she didn't think it was at all funny anymore.

The pressure was on.

"It's me or the business. You're supposed to be winding down now, not ramping up," she said, good to her ultimatum of three years earlier.

When you and your spouse are not aligned in your professional goals, you can have completely opposite reactions to the same set of events. For example, as we grew Audigy and started gaining more and more customers and becoming more and more profitable, we felt immensely proud of what we were accomplishing as a team. We were economically winning. We were changing people's lives. We had so many clients we loved, and it felt like we were helping them. We were creating new things and developing new business models and strategies. And I had bigger-picture goals for my life—like building a hundred Audigys, because that's really what I wanted to do. Right? I was fixated on changing how businesses were built.

But all this success left Tammy feeling colder and colder toward me. To her, my behavior suggested that I cared more about my customers and making money than about our family. To be honest, my children probably felt the same way at times. I never felt this was true because I felt I would do anything for my family. But in reflection, I can see why she thought that. I was so excited about figuring out how to make Audigy work, seeing it happen, and witnessing the impact on people's lives that it became like a drug to me. I was spending more time solving my clients' problems and wasn't directing my energy toward our homelife or paying attention to Tammy and the kids. There were times when I would come home after traveling all week, have dinner with my family, and then work the phone until midnight, solving my clients' issues or saving their families from financial disruption.

Although Tammy was more career-oriented than my first wife, she was not an entrepreneur whose passion to create something was like a guiding light. Entrepreneurs generally love to work and are passionate about what they do. There is a lot of talk about work-life balance as an important quality, but I believe the entrepreneur's guiding light is passion and total commitment, not balance. This is not a bad state of mind in which to exist. There is nothing to apologize for when you love what you do so much that it feels like play—or better than play, since it challenges you to achieve more than you dreamed possible, all while helping improve people's lives.

I would run in front of a car to save anybody in my family, including my ex-wives, and I live each day acutely aware that my obligation is to take care of my family—past and present—and to do so the only way I know how to, which involves building revolutionary businesses that help people who are not in my family as well those who are. With that said, my obligation is not to conform to anyone else's vision of what they want me to be. In the long run, being untrue to yourself never fulfills your purpose and only leads to frustration, which invariably damages your personal and professional life.

There was no way I was giving up on my life's dream, and there was no way Tammy was going to be married to someone she felt wasn't aligned with her.

But, to be fair, you can't count on those around you—even those you love and who love you—to share this perspective after the fact. Alignment has to be baked into a marriage from the start. Much as my experience in Atlanta had taught me to value professional independence as a nonnegotiable condition for my work, the failure of my second marriage taught me never to assume that my personal life would simply "work itself out" with respect to my professional life. This is especially true when you bring three amazing daughters into the world—like my Samantha, Brianna, and Ciara—who equally have to suffer the consequences of a divorce. From then on, if I entered into a new relationship with someone, it would be with both pairs of our eyes wide open to what we wanted from each other, our marriage, and our careers.

▪ ▪ ▪

Natalie Workman was an intern in my company, and I was very close to her family. She left to study at the London School of Economics and returned in 2015, when I was busy trying to launch a reverse consolidation company in the dental industry. I was also in the process of looking to sell Audigy.

My big hurdle in the dental industry involved the ninety point-of-sale systems that we tried to consolidate. I went to a third party, considered to be the only company in the industry that could aggregate all ninety offices into one data pipeline. I had spent a million dollars to license the technology and had hired a technology and operations team to go into each of the dental practices to make our system and scaling processes automated. The brilliant idea—emphasis on *idea*—was to create a system configured to optimize a business no matter what system it operated on, without having to convert it from one system to another.

That was the thesis, anyway. I believed in it enough that I stuck with it for five years and sank $8 million into the project. If it had worked, we could have added ten thousand dental practices online without needing to hire any more staff. Natalie returned to work with us, along with a couple of my long-term executives. They all worked hard on the project. It was a moon shot. Had it worked, it would have been huge. But it didn't work, thanks in part to our technology vendor's ineptitude and inability to deliver on their promise.

In 2017, it was Natalie who made the call to pull the plug before we lost any more money. At this point, Natalie had proven herself both intellectually and culturally by heading up two complex projects. On top of that, she loved the same people I loved. She liked working with people. She was so nice that it was disarming. I saw her as someone who could run a business in five or ten years, because people liked and respected her. When you're a street fighter, you get pretty good at sizing up talent in other people. In my career, I've spotted dozens of superstars, and Natalie was one of them. As she got into business, it was easy to see the fire in her to succeed. She handled herself beyond her years.

The three words that immediately came to mind when I thought about Natalie were, and continue to be, "smart, kind, and beautiful."

In September of 2015, after we'd been spending a lot of time together, I asked her whether she thought our friendship was becoming, well, more than friendship. Our friendship had been purely platonic, but it had become tinged with great affection. *Had we moved beyond friendship to something more serious?* I asked her.

After I posed the question about our relationship, Natalie was quiet for a moment. Then she smiled and said, "Yes." We agreed we'd better go tell her mom.

When we started dating in September of that year, it was hard for Natalie to assert herself in the business. She was much younger than me, and much younger than the members of my Audigy leadership team. She was also relatively unproven. As a businessperson, I am fast-talking and fast-thinking; it can be intimidating to people, especially to someone much younger—and when you have founded a company and served as its CEO, you're the boss at work, regardless of whether you and your wife are equals at home.

Of course, there were rumors we had to deal with about our motives for being together. Frankly, we grew so tired of having to explain ourselves to everyone all the time that we created a YouTube channel and podcast called *Age Gap Realness* to educate people on what falling and staying in love with someone much younger or older than you can entail. This was especially important to us given all of our family, friend, and community connections.

We didn't sugarcoat anything. In the first episode, Natalie shared how difficult it was to find her identity in our relationship because of the age gap.

"I am a confident person. I can walk into any room and talk with almost anyone," she said. "But I really struggled with my identity. And it was a painful struggle."

I remembered the period clearly and hearing her recall it caused me to tear up, right there on YouTube. But I managed to pull myself together enough to make the point that living in fear, anxiety, and stress compounds insecurity and drives a wedge deeper and deeper between couples. Recognizing what is happening is the first step, yet the stress makes recognition a difficult proposition at best. One of the things that makes Natalie and me such a strong, supportive couple is that our relationship was forged under pressure. Whereas many couples tend to fall apart under pressure, we thrived and grew stronger.

We also talked about money, since many people believe the stereotype of the younger gold digger marrying the older person for money. The role of money in an age-gap relationship is actually a bit more complex. I've come to believe that money amplifies a person's character, for good or ill. If the person entering a relationship with a wealthy individual is generally a fearful person or one who lacks confidence, those qualities will be amplified, not mitigated, by wealth. The broader lesson here is that it's far more important to know who you are than to listen to what others call you. Their opinions are not only based in ignorance but also completely, absolutely beside the point.

Know thyself.

By the time several dozen episodes of *Age Gap Realness* had been produced, Natalie had begun doing the show herself and enlarged the show's purview to include the general topic of self-awareness. The series is still available to view on YouTube.

▪ ▪ ▪

In my previous two marriages, I had been ignorant of the importance of alignment. Based on those failures, this time around I was not going to commit to someone who didn't want to go all in and have the same personal and professional and financial goals that I had. Natalie and I made sure we shared the same vision for what our life would be and the same values for how we'd live our life together. Outside of having three remarkable, healthy kids, plus grandkids, marrying Natalie was the single greatest thing that has happened to me in my life. We are comrades, colleagues, and best friends in every sense of the word. And we are fighting together for the things we both want rather than fighting against each other.

I reached the place where experience meets wisdom, and I found that perfect partner. Looking back at my previous relationships, I am far from sure I was the perfect partner to my wives. In fact, I am certain that my desire to succeed at times overshadowed my responsibilities and connection at home with my family. Being out of alignment with your spouse is a recipe for catastrophic results. One thing is for sure, I am not going to make that mistake again.

■ ■ ■

We often talk of breaking points that occur in the life cycle of running or growing a business. These inflection points can be personal, professional, or financial when it comes to building your business. They are moments that require new decisions, a new mindset, new systems and operational structures, and new talent to manage the growth. Failing to build in these systems and hire the right people can lead to an otherwise successful business's failure as it outgrows its founder's ability to lead it.

A different, but not unrelated, breaking point can occur in a business owner's personal life, such as in marriage, when the professional demands or passions of the business fall out of alignment with the spouse for whom the business is not a passion. This is a fact of business ownership that I've coached my clients on—and I've probably rescued a dozen or so client relationships in the last few years. As with my lessons learned as a business leader, I want people to learn from my challenges as a spouse so they can use what I've learned to handle the same problems better.

One way I do this is by taking a page out of Elena Cardone's book *Build an Empire*, in which she has couples go through an exercise that I recommend to our business partners as well. The exercise involves sitting down with clients, many of whom are married couples who run a family business, and giving them a piece of paper. I have them draw three columns: in the right-hand column, the husband lists his interests and focus; the wife lists her interests and focus on the left; and the middle column is left empty to allow the husband and wife to populate it with shared interests and needs. They often have to work harder than you might think to come up with items to put in the shared column, but they usually wind up talking about money, kids, vacations, or buying a house.

This starts to frame the conversation around things that can be created together. "I just want to have two weeks a year when we can just go away," says the wife, to which the husband replies, "I know, but my business is consuming me, and you know that I'm pushing for the family." You get them to identify what things in the middle column they can agree on. Then you get them to prioritize the items in the middle column and, perhaps, rearrange a few items on the left and right. Before you know it, you are ready to ask them, "If we could show you how to do these things, would you guys be committed to focusing on that and doing whatever you need to do to keep your relationship and business together?"

This technique may seem impersonal and technical, but it works. When I counsel business partners or couples, I recognize that when things get emotional, they are going to blame one another for whatever problems they are facing. And, in my experience, when there's high emotion, there's low intelligence. Most problems we encounter while scaling a business are technical, so I get the couple to displace their interpersonal blame onto the technical processes of scaling. Our conversation might go like this.

"If you had everything you wanted in your life, your spouse was coming home, and you could do your three or four vacations a year and you had the things that you want to have, would you feel the way you feel right now?"

"Of course not."

"Okay, so if you could feel better, then you'd be in a completely different place. True or false?"

"Absolutely true."

"Well, that's great. So either you're going to be controlled by momentum and struggle or you're going to struggle to control what you want. Either way, struggle is something you have to align with and agree to, so you have to agree on whether you want the struggle to work for you as a couple or you will let it pull you apart."

"We'd rather have it work for us."

"Okay, now let's move to the question of how you get your struggle to work for you."

Then we review the areas of their business and personal lives that will require struggle. They're going to struggle with building a team because they don't know how to build one; they're going to struggle with finding other people to come into the business and allow the couple to offload some day-to-day responsibilities. After assessing where their struggles lie, the couple may need to take as long as twelve months to fix the parts of the business that are broken.

Next, we put into place some milestones or markers—personal, professional, and financial. And as long as we're working toward those milestones, their confidence is going to go up about what they can create together. It's a profound pleasure to see this process open doors to a way out of the space they're trapped in. I know what it feels like to find your perfect life partner. Sometimes it's someone new in your life; other times, it can be someone you've known forever.

And if you can get in front of this fast enough, the perfect life partner can certainly and preferrably be the one you're already married to.

For additional resources, get immediate access to exclusive behind the scenes videos that uncover even more items I couldn't share in this book.
To access these exclusive resources, visit NineFigureTools.com

CHAPTER 9

Our New Chapter: Cardone Ventures

After selling Audigy, I was financially independent. I wouldn't have to work another day of my life if I didn't want to. The challenge was that I wanted to—work, that is. I didn't want my life to consist of little else than golfing, dining, and traveling around the world doing more golfing and dining. Natalie felt the same way, so we entered into a second sabbatical that differed from the one I'd undergone with Hector. During that earlier period, I'd needed to learn how to stop seeing myself as a victim and become a leader. Building and selling Audigy cemented that transition once and for all. Now, my problem was that I had voluntarily entered the ranks of the nonworking. It was not a place I wanted to be yet, nor did Natalie, who still felt she had so much to offer as a business leader herself.

Just as we had for all of our life together, Natalie and I decided to do some personal, professional, and financial goal-setting (PPF) to help us decide on our next project. We looked at our one-, five-, and ten-year goals. For myself, I had spent the better part of twenty years and millions of dollars creating a business model, accumulating the data, and reverse engineering hundreds of marketplaces and industries to build a business that could help the small to midsized business owner in a $12 trillion marketplace.

I had to ask myself whether I had what it took to start from scratch and begin grinding again. After going through the PPF process with Natalie, I decided the answer was "Absolutely!" When Natalie and I assessed where we were in our lives and where we wanted to go, we came up with a rather focused and practical list of five shared criteria. It made total sense, but would never have surfaced as a possibility had we not disciplined ourselves to do the PPF.

First, we needed a mentor or mentors who could furnish an example of what could be done—someone who had achieved the kind of success we wanted to achieve. Financially, I had always had the goal of reaching $500 million in net worth, so that narrowed our pool of mentors. Both Natalie and I wanted to work with someone whose expertise complemented mine rather than duplicated it, which could create friction and redundancy. We also wanted someone or *someones* who we could have fun with, because we are both people who like to work hard and play hard. We wanted to join forces with another couple who had made work and marriage a source of joy and accomplishment in their relationship. We wanted a couple similar to Natalie and me, who loved to build businesses as much as we did—in other words, who weren't simply trying to make enough money to exit.

Natalie is a voracious reader, which I am not, and also an avid consumer of news and online content, so she did a ton of research. Natalie read Elena Cardone's book *Build an Empire: How To Have It All*, and both of us read Grant Cardone's *The 10X Rule: The Only Difference between Success and Failure* and *Sell or Be Sold: How to Get Your Way in Business and in Life* and discovered two people who felt like soulmates to us. They had even developed their own version of the couple's goal-setting exercise Hector had introduced to me.

I could certainly see why Natalie thought Elena—an actress, author, and businesswoman—would make an ideal mentor, but I was less convinced, at least at first, about Grant. He was certainly a model of success: He owned five privately held companies with annual revenues above $100 million. He was the CEO of the top sales training platform in the world and consulted with Fortune 500 clients such as Google, Northwestern Mutual, Morgan Stanley, and others. He had mastered the art of investing in the multifamily real estate sector and had a portfolio of more than 3,800 apartment units throughout the US, with transactions valued at over $900 million. He was all over the place on social media and had created the first online entrepreneur and business TV network, Grant Cardone TV. You couldn't argue with the sheer size and number of his accomplishments.

But I had a serious bias against those I called "the social media guys."

"Ah, they're all full of crap," I told Natalie, who had signed us up to go to events featuring two of the couples we were researching—Tony Robbins and his wife, Sage, and Grant and Elena. "Look," I told her, "I don't want to walk on coals or do any of that stuff. I want to go do real business—not monkey business."

The first time she showed me Grant on YouTube, he was bopping around in front of his jet with his hat cocked sideways and was shooting money out of a cannon or something.

"There's no chance I will ever work with a guy like this," I repeated. "This goes against everything I stand for because he's just a promoter. This guy is like a bad cartoon character."

Undeterred, Natalie bought me audio versions of *The 10X Rule* and *Sell or Be Sold*, and brought them along on a three-hour car trip we were making to see my oldest daughter in Bend.

"We've got three hours of road time," Natalie said. "We're going to listen to Grant."

My fourteen-year-old daughter moaned from the back seat, and I moaned from the front seat, but we started listening. About thirty minutes into the audio, I started shaking my head and laughing because this guy knew exactly what he was talking about. My only regret was that I hadn't met him ten years earlier—although, truthfully, I had once had the opportunity to. One day, Mason told me he'd just finished reading a book by this guy who used to sell cars, which endeared him to Mason immediately. The guy's basic argument was that whatever you think is enough is probably ten times less than what you could do if you went all in on it and raised your expectations. The guy, who of course was Grant, had done it, and so could others.

"What does a car guy know?" was my enlightened reply.

Well, karma works in mysterious ways. A decade later, I found myself determined to meet the man who had suddenly given me a new perspective on life. His whole mantra that "success was a duty" that entailed "massive effort" and "belief in what you're selling" was absolutely my gig. So Natalie and I decided to attend Grant's 10X Growth Conference in Miami in 2019. We wanted to learn five very specific things.

First, did Grant's audience fit the kind of businesses we wanted to work with based on our research? Second, were Grant and Elena the real deal? Third, could we complement one another's strengths? Fourth, did Grant and Elena really work *together*? Natalie and I were looking for mentorship in working together. And finally, could Grant teach me how to achieve my goal of having a $350–$500 million net worth? We showed up at the conference and in the first half of the first day, we had checked all five boxes.

There are multiple lessons here. One, never be closed-minded. Second, always be prepared and do your homework on defining your intention. The more intentional you are, the easier it is to spot your opportunity. The story about meeting Grant and Elena shows the law of attraction playing out in real time.

People like Grant, who are extremely determined and focused and who become famous, often attract a lot of people who want to partner with them any way they can. Grant was no exception and had entered into various partnerships with people who let him down. As a result, he had built a fairly thick concrete fortification around himself when it came to any new partnerships. Fortifications can help protect you, but they can also work against you when they scare away opportunities to which you might be perfectly suited.

The more I thought about Grant, the more I felt we would be ideal business partners. So I wanted to set up Natalie and my introduction into his environment in a way that showed we were big thinkers like he was, yet knew how to have fun and make a splash in the ritual of business courtship. First, we bought $30,000 worth of Growth Conference tickets without telling anybody else. I went online and looked at the seating chart for the coliseum, which held about thirty-five thousand, and picked seats for Natalie and me that directly faced center stage, in a row that stuck out from the other rows; anybody looking out from the stage would see Natalie and me.

To make sure we registered with Grant as his gaze scanned the audience, I wore a pair of sparkly Louis Vuitton shoes that would positively explode with color when the lights swept over us. We wanted to be seen, but we didn't necessarily want anybody to know who we were until we were confident that Grant was working in the same neighborhood we wanted to work in—in other words, that he was teaching people things that would help them. Once we confirmed this, we wanted to introduce ourselves properly.

When it comes to introducing yourself to someone you want to form a relationship with, it pays to leverage your resources. In this regard, the person who makes the introduction can be as important, or more important, than the introduction itself. In the case of Grant, our only mutual friend happened to be John Maxwell.

"Who's the sharp-dressed guy with the beautiful wife?" Grant asked John after John finished his talk from the main stage and pulled Natalie and me up to the side of the stage to talk to us and try to introduce us to Grant. But because of the security situation and the show itself, it was impossible for them to meet at that moment. But the Louis Vuittons had done their work!

We kept our cool and eventually met Grant and Elena, but we also kept things light and never mentioned our long-term purpose. We wanted to send a message that we were there to learn and that our egos weren't so big that we couldn't learn something new. Besides, everybody was asking him to sign copies of his books, and the last thing he needed was somebody pitching him on forming a partnership.

I followed up with Grant in the months to come, and before long we began talking in earnest about the idea of forming a partnership. When Grant, Elena, Natalie, and I started having conversations, Grant and I quickly realized how complementary our skill sets actually were. We are very similar in how we think about business, which is to say we're both strategic thinkers who love to put systems and processes in place. We're also very methodical. He's also very savvy about marketing. But the key difference is that Grant is the greatest sales trainer in the world, and while I'm a pretty good salesperson, I've never put the discipline into sales that he has.

What I have developed expertise in is operationalizing companies quickly, effectively, and with no outside investment needed. My expertise was across ten separate elements: strategy, marketing, sales, people, finances, operations, leadership, data, technology, and investment thesis. It became very clear to me that Grant and I shared three of those elements and that I complemented him in the other seven.

In joining forces, I told Grant, I would blend everything smoothly together to be consistent. I never pitted my way of doing things versus his. On the contrary, I would fold all my research, experience, technologies, and methodologies into Grant's message of building a 10X business. In a nutshell, I told Grant I could give his 10X programs 360 degrees of applicability across the entire range of starting, scaling, and eventually exiting high-value businesses.

Coming from the audiology industry, I was relatively unknown in Grant's world, where he was generally recognized as one of the world's greatest sales coaches. From the start, I made a decision to be Charlie Munger to Grant's Warren Buffett. Munger is Buffett's right-hand man and 50 percent partner in Buffett's Berkshire Hathaway. Munger is far less known than his famous partner, but he is very capable—and very rich. I've never put my name on any of my companies because I never felt they'd be big enough, but I will always be okay being the Charlie Munger.

This was one of the reasons Grant, Elena, Natalie, and I were able to become partners with relative ease. As I mentioned, people who are as famous and successful as Grant have to put up with lots of characters who are trying to make money off of them. But my approach to building relationships is very slow and deliberate, built not on an effort to horn in on someone else's brand and success, but rather to tuck in behind them to provide incredible value and momentum through collaboration. That's the only way I know to build trust. The last thing Grant needed was for me to tell him how to be successful; truth be told, we needed Grant to help us 10X our personal, professional, and financial lives.

Early in our partnership, Grant asked me how much money I would need to launch our 360 Management company. I told him I needed nothing. I could build our model without raising or investing any money, using the same principles I was going to teach all our clients. In fact, one of the core lessons I taught at Audigy—and which we have now begun teaching at Cardone—is how to grow without using anybody else's money or needing capital or debt, because my overall expertise is getting the business to fund its own operations and growth.

"All I need for you to do," I told Grant, "is introduce me to the thousands of small business owners who come to your events, work with me to incorporate your marketing and sales expertise into my programs, and help me personally think bigger so I can do more."

Grant's reply was classic: "Okay, let's see if people buy your bullshit!"

Coming from anyone else, that might have seemed like an insult. But Grant is Grant and has earned the right to call 'em like he sees 'em. I think he saw me as a very good bet.

So Grant introduced me at one of his programs and invited me to present at one of his workshops. Both of us were thrilled to see the incredibly high level of enthusiasm for a business management component to complement Grant's sales-marketing program and real estate investment program. From then on, there was no looking back. With Natalie and I he had a business management company that could develop vertical business models for different industries—insurance, real estate, health care, equipment leasing, HVAC, logistics, cyber security, dentistry . . . you name it. Once we get ten or so businesses in a given vertical, we ask our best-performing clients to become partners and run a management company under Cardone Ventures for that vertical under the auspices of Cardone Enterprises as its partner.

In just around thirty-six months since we joined forces, Cardone Ventures has grown exponentially—to the point that neither Grant nor I hesitate to talk about a company worth billions.

The goal of our business model is to help one million 10X business owners to succeed. We do this by educating and then engineering their business case, giving them the blueprint for profitable and high-value growth. Then, for those who lead, we offer to become their partner and exchange equity in our management group for equity in their company, thus aligning our personal, professional, and financial interests.

Remember, the goal is not to sell them, but to help them grow and realize their dreams—we just take a management fee and a percentage of their upside we help them create in their business. In return, they own a piece of our new management company as long as they stay with us. This means they receive passive income in the form of regular dividends from our real estate holdings. Our relationship works more like a partnership than a strict client-consultant arrangement.

■ ■ ■

Natalie's research and instincts about Grant and Elena once again showed how insightful and savvy she is. Partnering with Grant and

Elena is proving not only the perfect next step for me personally, professionally, and financially, but also for Natalie. And it happened in large part because we sat down and did all of the important up-front work of examining our personal, professional, and financial goals—individually and as a couple. This included what we loved to do and hated to do and what we wanted out of our personal and professional lives.

We have learned so much from Elena Cardone as well. Natalie and I spent a lot of time working through the challenges of being so far apart in age as well as working together in the same company. But Elena literally wrote the book on how to build and fortify personal relationships in her book *Build an Empire: How to Have It All.* The level of mutual support she advocates for business-owning couples is something I blended into my own learning and teaching.

We're working as closely together as ever, with Natalie as president of Cardone Ventures, focusing on the operational and human resources aspects of our business. I handle the business development side of the business. Natalie hired practically all of our initial staff. She's stepped back from much of the direct recruitment, but has developed expertise in identifying and managing talent, including the R3 Assessment tool that measures our core energies and the things that motivate us. Some of the most enthusiastic participation in our 10X 360 workshops comes during the session when we discuss different personality types and which ones work the best, and the worst, together.

At the 10X 360 we take our clients through a two-day process based on all of the research and development I did on thousands of businesses from 2009 to 2017 with both FTI Consulting and IGS Consulting. Our research force ranked business growth conditions, consolidations, disruptions, and converging marketplaces to extract precise value in growing and scaling a business. In addition, we identified where businesses break or fail in the growth process. We created a data set that gives us the business blueprint on decision-making, process, and direction to engineer and construct the method for a business owner to maximize growth and value creation based on both this data and my business-building techniques and experience.

Business owners streamline their operations, financial results, people, technology, and data to accelerate their success and shore up any "hanging chads" that could cause the business to lose value or be damaged due to the lack of having a solid strategy, people foundation, or structure in place.

▪ ▪ ▪

The goal of Cardone Ventures is to help people all over the world take control of their destinies. We bring scale to the masses. We exist to help business owners break through the mistakes they will inevitably make, just as I did, and try to grow their companies from a 360-degree perspective. This perspective includes sales, operations, marketing, finance, and people. Every business owner formed a mental picture of their ideal place in the world before their brains got absorbed in the daily operations of running their business. Cardone Ventures helps them move toward that vision faster than they thought possible.

That's our mission. However, our mission differs from my legacy, which is how I want to end this book. My legacy defines what I want to be remembered as, not only through my close association with Cardone Ventures, but also by my dreams, my hopes, and my life. I should say *lives*, because I feel I've lived several lives, involving so many people I will never forget.

Well, here goes.

In the introduction to this book, I told you I wanted to conclude with the same challenge with which I opened, which was the challenge to ask yourself whether you had the resilience needed to overcome your fear of failure and make success an obligation in your life. When I think about what I hope my legacy consists of, it is that you will answer with a resounding "yes!" and find the hope and courage to seek what you want in life. I want people to remember me as the guy who helped them cut through the BS and get stuff done, hit targets, and live fulfilled.

I don't think people will think of me as their spiritual guru or anything like that. I want to be known as a guy who was on the side of the small business owner who felt trapped or afraid (or limited in some other way) until they met me or read my book and discovered a way of thinking and believing in themselves that pushed them to succeed faster, bigger, and better. I want to stand up for the mom-and-pop businesses whose founders work for thirty years only to have someone buy their business and flip it for ten times more money because they know how value works. My legacy is to be remembered as that guy, Dawson, who opened up a whole new world for a lot of hardworking people.

But I don't want to be thought of in isolation. Natalie and I want to leave a shared legacy—how we helped people together, built an amazing business that we loved, and enjoyed a beautiful life. I want to be remembered as part of the amazing community of people who have been with me on this journey—my mom and pop, my brothers and sister, my friends and mentors, the colleagues and clients I've met along the way—and who should know that I feel are a vital and living part of who I am.

And if we haven't met yet? Well, let's get to work.

For additional resources, get immediate access to exclusive behind the scenes videos that uncover even more items I couldn't share in this book. To access these exclusive resources, visit NineFigureTools.com

PART II

Conversations You Need to Have with Yourself

CHAPTER 10

Become an Expert on Yourself

Far too many people, including many of the entrepre-neurs I have spoken to over the years, spend too much of their short time on this blessed planet doing what they have come to believe they *should* do or must do, rather than what truly excites them and lights them up. Do you remember Henry David Thoreau's observation in *Walden* that the "mass of men live lives of quiet desperation?" That was 1854, and you know what? It's still true. They don't pursue a pathway that would bring them not only the financial rewards they seek but also the deep feelings of joy and fulfillment in their purpose.

It's trendy these days to talk about our "whys" and try to connect whatever line of work we're in with somehow making the world a better place. But just because something is on-trend—and not always followed up on by those who talk about it—doesn't mean that it doesn't contain a powerful lesson for us.

This is because our "why" doesn't have to involve making the world a better place in a broad or abstract way; it can and should mean making your own world and life a better place to live in. When I first told people that I was quitting my job with my family business and starting my own company, I heard the same things over and over again about why I should just "get a new job" or that I should have "remained satisfied with what I had." People told me this even though they knew the work was no longer bringing me joy or allowing me to pursue my true passions. I was fortunate, as I hope the first part of this book showed, to find a way to take full advantage of the incredible opportunities this life of ours has to offer. I count myself one of the fortunate ones who chose to embrace change, didn't fear the new and uncomfortable, wanted more out of life than, perhaps, I had been raised to expect, and recognized when an opportunity came along in the form of the right mentor who could push me to become a better version of myself.

To be completely transparent, I see more founders choose change as a last resort or out of desperation, which deprives them of enjoying the benefits that come from being proactive, putting their destiny in their own hands from the start, and enjoying the rewards that come with this autonomy.

The truth is that if 70 percent of your days are filled with activities that don't align with your own core values and don't bring you joy or excitement, the remaining 30 percent can't compensate for that. In fact, the more time you spend doing things that aren't satisfying to you, the more money you'll spend on other things, such as hobbies and vacations, in an effort to compensate for your growing unhappiness. The result is that you will become more and more tied to doing work that you dislike in order to pay for your compensatory habits. Life is too short to live for weekends, my friend.

SELF-DISCOVERY INCREASES YOUR PERSONAL POWER

I often hear people say, "I want to explore my inner self, my thoughts and emotions, but I'm afraid of what I'm going to find." I understand this fear, but no matter how terrible the truth may be, it's powerless in itself to harm you. Your fear is caused by your resistance to learning the truth—the things you don't want to face or change because they have felt comfortable for so long. To become a better version of yourself, you must be willing to struggle a bit, to discover the good, the bad, and the ugly within and accept them as part of who you are now. Don't judge them, simply accept them—though not as a life sentence that you will be forced to serve out no matter what you do.

The faster you can release judgment of yourself and others, the faster you can proceed from a rational and sensible viewpoint. That viewpoint begins with understanding that we are always learning and growing. There's simply no end to it. Learning and growing is a daily practice you must commit to now in order to give yourself grace through the process of doing work that has the potential to change your life. The reason most people don't do the work is because it's hard and often not fun. It brings up triggers and memories and life experiences from childhood that we need to heal—or hide—from.

I have used, and will continue to use, the word *opportunity* in this book because I believe that the world is bursting with opportunities for those who are willing to open themselves up to change. But I don't believe that every opportunity is the right opportunity for every person. Many people think they can spiritually bypass the stage of self-discovery and that things will somehow just work out when the right opportunity comes along.

That's not how finding your purpose works. Nothing but good can come from being on a journey of self-discovery. Don't concern yourself with whether you're better or worse than other people or on a different timeline from friends and family. Don't waste your energy and time dwelling on your shortcomings or failures. They are all there for a purpose. All of them. It's never easy to make sense of the various strands of life in the moment, as they are being woven into who we are, but the dots will eventually connect and it will all make sense. Be patient and gentle with yourself. You only get to where you want to be by accepting where you are right now.

The goal is not perfection, it is progress.

As an example, you wouldn't look at a building that's under construction and condemn it for being unfinished, right? Adopt this way of thinking about yourself and your business. Whatever your present condition, just realize that you are a marvelous work in progress with a huge opportunity for growth.

As we discussed earlier, over the years I've used the term *entrepreholic* to describe the many business owners I met who were afraid to admit an important but uncomfortable truth about their relationship to their business. This relationship was preventing them from moving toward the goals and dreams they truly wanted. Entrepreholism is a state of being addicted to doing things that are less and less satisfying and which, as a result of being less and less satisfying, generate smaller and smaller rewards—emotionally, professionally, and financially. It is a mindset, a state of being in which one becomes closed to thinking outside of what one has always known. An entrepreholic is somebody who relates to his business the same way alcoholics relate to alcohol: They think they have to imbibe constantly. They see no way out.

That's why, as business owners and leaders, we have to embrace the imperative that honesty is the best policy: honesty about who we are, what we truly want, and why we haven't tapped our true abilities to achieve a massive impact. Albert Einstein said the definition of insanity was doing the same thing over and over again and expecting different results. All of us have been guilty of this kind of insanity at some point in our lives, haven't we? We all do the same things over and over again, even though we know they don't work. Many of the business owners I have interviewed over the years concede that they do it. They haven't moved closer to their goals, but they're unwilling to change what they do and how they do it.

Self-discovery requires that we admit to ourselves what isn't working. It's the first step in making changes. Through self-discovery, you will find personal, professional, and financial freedom. Hector

LaMarque had agents who made $50,000 per year and agents who earned millions of dollars per year. Some of the highest earners were new agents who had only been on the job for five or six years. I experienced the same syndrome in my business. One employee generated $1 million per year in sales, while most made $200,000–$500,000.

One day, I asked Hector, "What's the difference between the ones who do really well and the ones who make an average amount of money?"

His answer was short and crystal clear, as usual.

"Well, Brandon, it's easy. The difference is simply how they think and what they do."

Self-discovery is the start of understanding how you think. And when you change how you think, you will change what you do.

BECOMING AN EXPERT ON YOURSELF

Everything you learn about yourself is good news. Even the stuff that seems unflattering. Exposing what we perceive as our weakness marks the beginning of turning a weakness into a new strength. No matter how difficult or surprising it may be, this dynamic always creates the opportunity for good news. Learning how to detach from the emotion of the information and not beat yourself up over it will be crucial. The key is not to identify with your faults *or* with your virtues. Don't see them as the things that define you now and forever, but as negative habits, behaviors, beliefs, and values you can change into positive ones with the right focus and determination. Observe your strengths and weaknesses without judgment and without pride.

You should see a weakness as it is, without judging it but also without excusing it or justifying it. View it as a part of your personality that you want to improve. Don't allow yourself to feel paralyzed by a weakness—that will prevent you from learning how to think and do something new. Being open and honest with yourself in this way will preserve you from the complacency of identifying with your strengths as well as from a harmful, self-limiting identification with your mistakes, faults, and errors.

When I teach business owners and leaders how to speed this process up, I teach them the power of the "four A's." When you're up against a challenge, a risk, fear, anxiety, or stress and you're trying to break through, apply the four A's. First, *acknowledge* where you're at; next, *accept* where you're at; then *act* in the direction you want to go; and, finally, as you gain momentum, *attack* it.

One of the traits of highly successful people is that they commit themselves to never stop learning, growing, improving, and (as I learned from Grant Cardone) multiplying. They realize that life is a journey rather than a destination and that incremental, continuous improvement is where the fun lies, not on some imaginary beach, sitting in a lounge chair and drinking piña coladas. The first thing to do is make changes in yourself. Once you are an example to others, apply those same changes within your organization and within your people. This is how you multiply, amplify, and ultimately scale your business.

The biggest mistake I see inexperienced business leaders make is failing to inspire others to make the same changes. You need to be an example first, because those who can't "do" won't be an example to others. I believe in the laws of attraction, but attraction only occurs after you've followed the laws of intention and action.

Let me explain.

WHAT TRULY BRINGS YOU JOY?

Successful, high-performing people determine what they want and build a pathway toward that end result. When was the last time you asked yourself what you really wanted, what made you a happy person? If money wasn't an object, what would you spend your days doing? How much time would you want to spend with your family and friends? How would you want to structure your day so that you could show up as the best version of yourself? Write these answers down.

Everyone wants to feel good every day. We all tend to develop habits and pursue pastimes we believe will get us that good feeling, which suggests that in order for us to determine what we want, we need to know what we enjoy. But once you know the answer, reaching your goals will be much easier, and they will be so much more *fun* to go after. You'll be able to work backwards and design a plan to get you to where you want to be. Create a vision and believe you deserve it. This is a crucial piece in the process. You have to see it—actually visualize yourself and allow the thing you desire to energize you toward seeking its accomplishment.

Here's how I change my future picture. I go out ten years and visualize what I've accomplished. I visualize what people are saying about me. I visualize what people are writing about me in news articles and press releases. I visualize what they're saying about me at charitable organizations because of my donations. I visualize what people in the local community and the business community, my employees, my partners, and my customers are saying about the innovations I created. I see myself on the cover of magazines as the inventor of a new way to build businesses. I see myself flying in my fleet of planes, living the optimal life. I've got a beautiful yacht where I take my best customers and my most-valued partners. I feel, taste, and see these images over and over and over ten years out.

And then, in the moment when I'm under pressure and I'm uncertain of what to do, I ask myself whether the things I'm doing today are pulling me toward that ten-year vision or sidetracking me from it. And I make decisions that keep me pulling toward that vision. In this way, I replace the programming of my past experiences that make me reactive in my present with the new mental imagery of my ten-year self.

You must be the co-creator of your future. And the way to do this is to make decisions during moments of stress that reflect your ten-year image of yourself rather than your present self. Why should you do this? Your present self has been programmed based on all your past failures, people projecting onto you, the opinions of teachers, parents, churches, and the government, not to mention the impact of negative experiences on your belief in yourself. Your ten-year self wipes this slate clean and allows you to establish your intentions clearly and act in a way that brings your intentions to life, moment by moment, in the present.

Only then, after you have established a clear picture and are fulfilling your purpose and doing what you love to do, will you naturally attract the right resources and people and circumstances you need to help you accomplish your goal. That's the laws of intention, action, and attraction at work!

Once you do this, refine your vision by asking yourself why you want to create a future ideal scene—that picture of who you have become. What do you want to get out of it, including financial reward but also other things—having a team to lead, improving an important product or service, changing the world, adopting a cause, and so on. The more you can envision the massive impact you will have realized across your personal, professional, and financial life in ten years, the more you can actively shape your present to pull you toward that dream.

Once you start generating this new mindset every day, showing up to work will become a game, and your business will be your sandbox. Stake your claim by sharing your dreams with other people and letting them see who you have chosen to be. Act as if it has already happened.

One of the best ways to discover what you want is to start with creating a list of loves and hates. Write out a one-sentence answer beneath each question. For many of the business owners I work with, the answers can be as simple as, "I love doing the technical aspect of my work, seeing people, and working with technology." Or, "I hate doing the books, calling back upset customers, and dealing with my employees."

Love to do

What do you love to do in your business?

What are you passionate about?

What gets you out of bed in the morning?

What inspires you to go all in?

What excites you?

What do you want to create?

What thing are you best at?

Hate to do

What disappoints you?

What keeps you awake at night?

What makes you want to *stay* in bed in the morning?

What makes you procrastinate?

What do you wish you didn't have to do?

What fills you with regret?

What wastes your time?

Once you've created your lists, sit back and digest them for a while. Analyze them word for word. Pay attention to how each of the lists makes you feel. I think you'll see and feel quite a difference. If you're like me, the love list will make you smile and get your blood pumping, while the hate list will make you feel anxious and, perhaps, even a little nauseous.

Fill in the "hate to do" list with massive action!

23 IMPORTANT QUESTIONS TO ASK YOURSELF RIGHT NOW

Some people find it difficult to think about what they're passionate about or where their true talents lie. It's hard to know where to begin, and it can be difficult to simply pull such things out of thin air. Answering the following questions will give you some important data, which may help you focus and determine the path you want to take. Spend some time with each of these questions, answering them thoughtfully and truthfully—*and write them down*. That way, you can refer to them later or revise them as experience dictates. Remember, your talent should outweigh your "passion." Hitting your goals will be all the passion you need, so prioritize hitting your targets more than what you are passionate about.

Think 10X bigger and ten years out as you ask yourself *very specific* questions such as these:

1. What type of work do I want to do every day in my business?
2. What kind of lifestyle do I want to provide my family with?
3. What are my personal goals?
4. What are my professional goals?
5. How much money do I want to make?
6. How big do I want my company to be?
7. How do I measure success?
8. What do I want my employees to say about me?
9. What do I want my legacy to be? (What do I want to leave to the world, my family, my friends, my team?)
10. What do I want my customers to say about me?
11. What would my family say about my work-life balance?
12. What are my favorite hobbies or pastimes?
13. How do I prefer to volunteer my time?
14. What subjects do I enjoy going deep on with friends?
15. What do I daydream of more than anything else?
16. What have been my favorite job responsibilities?
17. What are my pet peeves?
18. What tasks in my business energize me the most?
19. What tasks in my business do I excel at above all others?
20. What tasks do I think I could excel at but haven't yet tried?
21. If I could start another company, would I? What would it be?
22. What kinds of people do I love to be with? Why?

23. Who do I most admire and why?
24. If I won $100 million, what would I do with it?
25. If money were absolutely no object at all, I had no practical considerations to take into account, and all possibilities were open to me, what would be the first thing I'd do in my business?

After you have completed your answers, read them again with an eye to comparing them to your love and hate lists. Can you tease out any patterns that you should pay attention to?

Review your commitment list again, and this time look for the items that involve escape. These are the things you do to avoid the things you dread. Don't mistake running *away* from unhappiness for running *toward* joy. We all have things we don't like to do or think we're not good at; *not doing them* isn't the kind of energizing, productive joy I'm talking about. Cross these items off your love list. They simply give you the temporary avoidance of pain.

Following your passion and abilities requires a series of incremental steps. This is another reason people have trouble thinking about what they're passionate about. Truth be told, it rarely comes as a single flash of insight; rather, it emerges as the gradual outcome of an effortful process of getting to know yourself better and asking, "If I put the same effort into finding what gives me joy as I put into doing what I dislike, why wouldn't I end up with results that will make me think, *Why did I wait so long to do this?*"

Why, indeed?

PEOPLE-PLEASING IS A PSYCHOLOGICAL DEAD END

I had to come to terms with the fact that for far too long, my business aspirations were solely motivated by trying to prove something to others and not based on what I truly wanted. Only when I discovered what I wanted, exclusive of anyone else, was I able to create a satisfying life and successful business that made me genuinely happy and grateful every day. And once I became happier and more grateful, I was a better person not only in my professional life but also in my personal life. It's harder to express loving-kindness to others when you don't feel it toward yourself, and looking for that affirmation in others' eyes is bound to disappoint.

Why? Well, the old saying that "you can't please everybody, so you have to please yourself" is true to the extent that you'll always be a failure in *someone's* eyes. People are simply too wrapped up in their own drama and relentless defense of their self-esteem and insecurities to take a deep interest in your self-esteem and overall worth. As likely as not, they are projecting some drama taking place in their own heads onto you. That's a play in which you don't want to have any role.

This is true even among family members. As I noted earlier in the book, I strongly counsel husbands and wives who want to go into business together to do the hard, up-front work of figuring out what each of them is most passionate about, as well as their "loves" and "hates," before going into business. Two people can be happily married yet have very different—and not necessarily compatible—goals and values when it comes to their professional lives. Of course, the opposite may be true: entrepreneurism may be yet another match made in heaven for them.

This is the reason I encourage all couples and prospective business partners to do the up-front work of going through the exercise we learned from Elena Cardone in her book *Building an Empire* to find out what matters most to each person as well as discovering where they are aligned in their personal, professional, and financial goals.

I also encourage you to be very careful in choosing the people you allow to influence you. If the person giving you advice has not succeeded in the kind of thing you're pursuing, find someone else to go to for advice. Find someone in your industry who has successfully done what you want to do. Find out what they believe, how they think, and what they did that led to their successful results. Then emulate their example. This is not being a copycat. It is being a life-long learner. There are very, very few original ideas under the sun, as the Good Book tells us, but there is infinite variation on those that do exist. Make one of them yours and own it.

If you're really going to learn the truth about yourself and your business, as well as live your life as fully as possible, you are bound to alienate some people who will resent the time and effort you put into your calling. Are you going to deny yourself riches and good health and loving relationships because others lack one or more of these blessings? If you are committed to *you*, the answer must be no. As we will discuss in a later chapter on developing your employees, a business leader has to model the mindset and actions he or she expects from others. And if you don't believe you have any right to live a life of abundance, well-earned by the sweat of your brow, how could you possibly expect others to believe they have that right and should listen to what you have to say?

An additional good reason to focus on your own values and passions—and how you see yourself in ten years—is that no one else is likely to enjoy your success and feel as deeply fulfilled by it as you. Others may see in you a reminder of their own failure to fully step into their own purpose and pursue their dreams. Success can be intimidating when it forces others to question their courage, skill, or ambition to create the life they desire. This is why people often try to convince you that something can't be done. When you prove it *can* be done, it can feel like a blow to their egos.

People who are insecure and don't know who they really are will always be frightened by the unfamiliar. Can you see how limiting it can be to not invite the process of self-discovery into your life? Learn to please yourself and enjoy who you are. Self-worth comes from self. That's why it isn't called "other-worth." If your worth comes from others, you will never be able to love yourself.

Finally, in discovering your journey in life and recognizing that you will not always be judged favorably by others—sometimes even by those you trust—do not return the favor and live a life reduced to judging others. To judge someone else is to destroy a little piece of their spirit, which in turn degrades a little piece of your spirit as well. Keep your spirit keyed to the abundance the world has to offer and you will attract abundance to yourself and those around you.

For additional resources, get immediate access to exclusive behind the scenes videos that uncover even more items I couldn't share in this book. To access these exclusive resources, visit NineFigureTools.com

Goal-Setting at FIT Solutions

Ephraim Ebstein, Owner

My business partner and best buddy and I started FIT Solutions in late 2012 as an IT service provider and expanded our services to include cybersecurity. We started it from nothing, and now FIT Solutions is celebrating its tenth anniversary as a company that serves small- and medium-sized businesses. During the early years, we grew to around $5 million, and our staff grew to more than forty. We were having a hard time making payroll and realized that if we were going to survive, we had to take our company to a whole new level with better systems and management.

I realized I had to do two things. First, I needed to improve my financial literacy. I'd always figured that if I provided excellent service to my customers, they would be loyal to us and everything would just fall into place. Clearly, there was more to being financially strong than that. The second realization involved sales: I was educated as an engineer and was very comfortable with the technical side of IT, but I needed to become a much better salesman for my company.

In the summer of 2017, I started watching Grant Cardone's You-Tube videos about selling and, before long, began attending his events and workshops. I also began to send my team to his events to increase our overall sales literacy. I met Brandon Dawson and immediately began working with him on a regular basis. One of the most useful things he taught us early on was to work through our goals on paper. Everyone in our organization did it, and do you know what? Most of us, including me, had a hard time writing our goals down on paper because, we discovered, we didn't know what we wanted to accomplish. Writing them down forced us to make decisions we'd never had the discipline to make.

As we worked through our goals, something dramatic happened. My business partner and I discovered that we had rather different goals for our personal, professional, and financial lives. He was getting more worn out by the grind, while I felt like we were just getting started and saw a long future with the company at the center of my life.

Through this process, Brandon helped both me and my partner part ways in a professional and honorable way through our goal-setting and helped us organize and construct the exit process so my partner could go pursue his goals while I pursued my goals of building the business. We're still best friends, which I'm thankful for. The clarity of goal-setting helped us achieve this resolution faster than we would have otherwise. It may also have prevented problems in our friendship down the road, even though we'd always enjoyed a great working relationship. Real goal-setting changed the trajectories of our paths. It changed our lives.

To provide a sense of just how different my trajectory is, my current ten-year goal is to reach $300 million in revenue. At present, most of our revenue comes from IT support; I see the bulk of our future growth coming on the cybersecurity side, where there is huge demand. Another advantage to our strategy of growing cybersecurity is that I don't have to put boots on the ground. In the cities where we provide IT support, we have to hire staff to live there.

One of the biggest breakthroughs we achieved working with Brandon involved creating and aligning with a mission and vision for FIT. Our mission is to impact lives through technology. And our vision is to help six thousand businesses achieve their goals through technology.

Our mission and vision allow us to widen the circle of who we impact to include not only our customers—the obvious ones—but also our staff and their families. When we started FIT, I thought about how cool it would be to succeed in building a company. Now, I see the business as something that helps not only me and my family have a better life, but also all of those who help make it happen. Those aren't just words. I've come to view the purpose of FIT in the broader context of making life better for lots of people. In fact, technology just happens to be the thing I'm good at, but it's less important to me than the larger mission.

This realization has made me appreciate what we do to a much greater degree than when it was all about the technology. But at the same time, it makes it easier for my employees and me to take care of the technology side—to be better at everything we do—because that is how we fulfill our mission and vision. In the past, when I spoke with employees about their goals, they usually kept it strictly professional: they talked about what they wanted in their careers. Rarely did we discuss what they wanted to do with their lives or even what financial goals they had.

Bringing these topics into the discussion shows them how their professional goals help them reach their personal and financial goals; it also lets them see how to align their efforts at work with the company's overall goals. Alignment can come down to something as direct and measurable as realizing that if we can improve our on-site efficiency by 1 percent, we will make more money as a company and our staff will earn more money in raises or bonuses.

Since we've begun this goal-setting process, two things have happened. First, everyone across the company is hitting their goals faster than they thought they would. The increased transparency that comes from aligning personal and collective goals has accelerated the rate at which goals get accomplished. Second, I'm noticing that our employees are thinking bigger in general. They are quicker to set up new and larger goals as older ones are being met faster. We're experiencing a winning culture that feels very positive.

People want to grow, and we're providing the means for them to do so.

We created a policy of asking everyone in the company to spend at least fifteen minutes each day training. Whether you're in sales or HR or accounting, you have the opportunity to invest in your development every day at FIT Solutions. This is not inexpensive at a company of our size. There are costs for the training content and the tools, but also for the time employees need to produce a result. For HR training in a new software platform, a result might be reducing the time needed to fill jobs; for engineering staff who work directly with clients on IT and security issues, billable time spent serving customers and customer satisfaction are two results we expect to see improve with training.

We incentivize these metrics with bonus plans. Brandon's team helped us develop an employee maturing model that shows what competencies and results employees need to demonstrate to move to the next position when it becomes available. Everything is transparent, so they can see, for example, exactly what it takes to move from engineer to senior engineer or from manager to senior manager. This takes the frustration and guesswork out of setting goals for promotion. I'm also up-front about my long-term goal of growing the company to $300 million. My employees know that this goal will create more opportunities for them to advance in their own careers and lives.

And here I have to go back to Brandon and Grant, who taught me that in order to 10X yourself, you have to set a goal that scares you a little bit because you're not sure how you could possibly do it. The great thing about 10X goals, however, is that even if you fall short, you're so much further along than if you played it safe. It just means you haven't gotten there yet. You only fail if you give up. If you haven't given up, you're still on the road to getting it.

You just have to keep going.

Vision: Aquatic Pools and Spas Learns a Concrete Lesson

Jacy Silva, Owner

When my husband, Thiago Silva, moved to America from Brazil, he went to work in his father's swimming pool construction company. Thiago has always been what I call a big dreamer—a visionary who loves to think about the big picture. I am completely different: I am very analytical and process-oriented.

After a short while, Thiago and I started our own pool construction company. We were very proud, but then one of our most important clients—we got our work from pool companies that sold residential pools in the South Carolina region—went out of business. We had to decide whether to open our own company to pick up the marketing and sales that were lost. So we opened a pool company called Aquatic Pools and Spas in addition to our construction business.

We did around $500,000 in our construction and pool sales businesses in our first year. Of course, the problem was that the other pool companies now saw us as competitors, so the flow of projects from them came to halt. We had to get better at selling our own services, so we did some research online and found a sales boot camp offered by Grant Cardone, which we attended in July 2019. A couple of months after the boot camp, we began working with Brandon Dawson, who showed us how every part of our business affected the other parts, and how young businesses have to prepare for growth.

One of the things Brandon's team helped us do was learn how to accept our different strengths as a team instead of letting them get in the way. Thiago is the big thinker, but he is also the driver and doer. He comes with the idea, and I think through the details to see how that idea is going to happen. We didn't always see eye to eye on decisions. I had to learn to trust his big visions. For example, the cost of working with Brandon's team was almost exactly what we had managed to save after years of hard work. We were still renting our house and wanted to be able to afford to buy our own home.

When we met Brandon, we had been doing $3 million in revenue and paying ourselves $125,000 a year for ten years, so I wasn't excited about investing our life savings in working with Brandon. But Thiago saw that Brandon was for real. He had been in the same position we were in and knew how to be successful. He was like Thiago—a visionary. Once we made the hard choice to invest in Brandon and have him help us build our business, the unimaginable occurred.

Brandon told us when we made that investment that we sell the way we buy and buy the way we sell. He said that once we released our fear of investing our last dollar in our business, we would open the opportunity for abundance to happen within our life. We made the investment and in our first year did over $8 million of revenue. Our second year we did $20 million in revenue. And our third year we did $33 million in revenue.

Our dream target was to have enough money invested in real estate that we'd have a passive income that allowed us to never have to worry about having a job again. We accomplished that goal within three years of working with Brandon. What accounted for the success? Well, it wasn't going to business school! It came from changing our mindsets to believing in our product and ourselves, not to mention believing in Brandon.

One of Thiago's visions was to set our product apart from our competitors by using concrete to build our pools rather than fiberglass or vinyl. Concrete lasts longer, requires less maintenance, and offers greater flexibility in terms of the shapes people want. The other materials are just delivered as giant tubs that you put in the ground.

When the company that sold us our concrete couldn't keep up with the demand for our pools, Thiago had the idea of starting our own concrete company. So we started a third business called Smart-Gunite. We bought six cement trucks at $240,000 apiece that served our pool business as well as our competitors. It was a big investment, but it is paying off and it will help us to grow when the time comes that we want to open new locations.

We have grown from five people—which included Thiago and me—to twenty-two people at our sales operation and concrete company. There are another thirty-two people who work at our construction company.

The change came because we believed nothing could prevent us from going where we wanted to go. When you think this way, you feel more confident that whatever problem arises, you can solve it. For example, as with the concrete company that had been slowing us down, we used to work with an electrician who had different ideas about how fast we wanted to go. We solved the problem by hiring our own in-house electrician. We make it a practice to never hire people just based on super credentials. We want people who have the right attitude for our company. For example, our director of sales, Benjamin Prillaman, used to be a youth pastor. He joined Aquatics as a project manager. He is a wonderful communicator, a quality which

Thiago saw in him, so we moved him into the sales side of the business. He has flourished there and now has a staff of seven.

Our team continues to participate in programs for coaching, sales execution, finance essentials, and leadership with Brandon and Grant. In our market, we are the fastest pool builder. It counts for a lot. Many construction estimates are ten months or more; we are much faster—often nearly twice as fast! As soon as you inquire on our website, you hear from us within an hour. We're much faster on the communication and outreach side of things. When someone calls us, we appreciate how much they want to hear back from us. These are habits we learned working with Brandon's team.

When we meet with customers, our salespeople break down estimates and point out possible delays and such that might come up during the project. We have found that even if a competitor's price is a bit lower, we can win the bid because people appreciate our level of transparency. They know why we charge what we do and what we offer. But they also want to know that we care about their satisfaction and are there for them.

Brandon's philosophy of business leadership is to model the values and behavior you expect, then teach your team to mimic this behavior. When they master it, they teach others in the company to do the same. This creates your company culture.

Brandon's team modeled what it was like to always be there for the customer and taught us how to always be there for ours. Now we are mastering this, and our customers are rewarding us by making us a leader in our marketplace. One of our mottos is "we want to make every day a vacation day for you." We are a living example of this philosophy. We believe you can do anything if you network with the right people and find your mentor, someone who has done what you have dreamed of doing and wants to teach you the steps to achieving your dream.

I am still the analyzer in Thiago's and my relationship and always will be more skeptical. But I have learned how powerful belief can be. Where I once fretted about losing everything, today Thiago and I have a house with horses and chickens and, of course, a nice swimming pool. We also have two children who keep us very busy during whatever free time we can find.

But it's all good. In fact, it's nothing less than a blessing.

CHAPTER 11

Your Beliefs Shape Your Business

When I started my first business, I was quickly able to see the impact of each employee's self-image and belief system. Many of my sales professionals believed that $250,000 was the most revenue a single practitioner could generate in a year. When I told them that they were capable of doing more, they usually said, "That's impossible," or, "Your expectations are too high."

I started a new program where we had our current, high-producing hearing care professionals train our new team members. Since the new sales professionals were trained only by those who regularly generated annual revenue of $600,000 to $1 million, the new people accepted those figures as not only achievable, but normal. They acted on this belief and thus were able to generate those same revenues for my company very quickly. Can you imagine the reactions of my longer-term employees who believed they were working "as hard and efficiently as possible"? Here were professionals with little to no experience earning more than twice what the long-term professionals had. It certainly stopped the excuses, and everybody's productivity went up. Creating a new belief about what can be done is a core practice with all the companies I have built and is the top job of a leader.

Whether your beliefs are realistic or completely nuts, they determine what your life and your business will be about. Richard Bach, author of *Jonathan Livingston Seagull*, said, "Argue for your limitations and sure enough, they're yours." Pronounce your business limitations vigorously enough, and they're yours.

The next time you're in a meeting whose topic involves how you might get the business to grow, notice whether the conversation eventually turns to arguing about all the reasons it *can't* grow. I'll bet you discover that words such as *doubt* and *reservations* and *not sure* and the most qualifying word of them all, *but*, as well as other self-limiting words crop up more and more during the conversation. Such meetings usually devolve from planning sessions into status quo sessions in which, one by one, people point out the obstacles standing in the way.

Pretty soon you'll forget about the new idea you wanted to try out as the old excuses pull the conversation back to old goals and objectives that haven't been met. When you are fixated on false beliefs, those beliefs create the very conditions of your limitations.

I once had a long-term client who was absolutely convinced that no matter what, his business couldn't do more than $250,000 per year. He would argue, fight, and entirely dismiss any suggestion otherwise. After thirty years in business, he called me and said his health wasn't very good and asked if I could help him sell his business. I called Matt and Jeff Wilken and put them together. We asked the guy's wife if she wanted to stay on after the acquisition and run the business, and whether she would be willing to have us teach her how to turn it into a million-dollar-a-year business? She said yes. Within a year of owning the business with the Wilkins, she did $1 million in revenue.

The point was that as long as the husband reinforced the belief that there was no way to do more than $250,000, he created the conditions to never do more than that amount. Once you establish a belief, even a false one, the job of the subconscious is to find information to fortify that belief. Then you create the conditions to "be right." Imagine holding a false belief for twenty-five years and then your wife proves you wrong in her first year of running the business without you!

What you believe creates the conditions for your success or failure. The problem is that many people would rather believe they are "right," even when confronted or challenged by alternate possibilities that make total sense, than commit themselves to change that makes them happy in the long run.

We tend to justify what's gone wrong in a situation rather than look for solutions. We live with a set of beliefs called politics, a set of beliefs called religion, a set of beliefs called "what our parents and teachers taught us," and a set of beliefs based on our own trials, tribulations, and failures. Each of these determines how we think about ourselves, our businesses, and our staff. We think our beliefs are the intrinsic truth. Yet many of our beliefs differ from the beliefs of others—who also think that *their* beliefs are the intrinsic truth.

Somebody has to be wrong, right? The desire for certainty is hardwired into our being to the point of becoming default settings, which is a technical way of saying they become beliefs.

"It failed twice before, so it will fail the next time we try it, regardless of how we do it," is a statement that speaks right from our amygdala, the part of the brain that stimulates our fight-or-flight response. It wants to protect us from the shame or depression of another failure or the fear of getting fired, but in doing so it is just as likely to limit us from trying something new that would have made us stronger and more valuable to our business than ever.

Every business owner who has worked with us over the years has come to us with a set of beliefs about what their businesses can do, what they can't do, and what their employees can and can't do, along with an ironclad certainty about what their market opportunity is. We have found that their beliefs are rarely well-founded.

Take Stacy and Gary Conner, the husband-and-wife founders and owners of Equipment Experts in Washington State. The company operates a fleet of repair trucks and provides on-site repairs to heavy equipment and vehicles. The concept was great, and Stacy and Gary had built the company from scratch, which meant growing from a single truck to a dozen or so when we began working with them. One of their problems was that they were having a hard time getting traction on a subscription program that they felt would improve their ability to generate high-quality repeat business.

Stacy dubbed the problem her "Jell-O wall," which she defined as "an invisible barrier we create for ourselves out of something we feel we should be able to do but can't and so settle unconsciously for 'can't.'" Their reaction to the problem had been to lower their sales targets—that is, until we worked with their team to figure out how they could better communicate their value proposition through the sales and service of subscriptions.

But before their professionals could learn to present the value proposition in a more compelling way, they had to adjust their belief in what was possible.

"Choosing to be negative is a decision point," Stacy told me. "You can fight for that negative point, or you can choose not to fight for the negative any more. And that is a really hard decision point to pivot on. But the more you fight for your beliefs and your dreams, the more the bad stuff—the negative—kind of melts away."

Another Jell-O wall Stacy and Gary had been fighting through involved cash flow, which is a critical piece of any company's success, especially during difficult times or crises. To date, Stacy is on track to hold cash covering up to 20 percent of her bottom line, something she'd never been able to come close to before but understands is important.

"I don't ever want to worry about whether we can stay in business during a crisis again," she said. "I'm choosing to believe we can do it rather than telling myself stories of why we can't."

Most people have a very hard time holding conflicting beliefs in their minds without experiencing anxiety or distress. Whenever we have a strong belief we think is true, we lock onto it as a defense against conflicting beliefs that induce anxiety. When pressed, we'll gather supportive data and information to prove we're "right," even when what we believe has nothing to do with the viability of a conflicting idea. Think about the last change you made in your business. Was it a change in your staff, product supplier, business line, or marketing campaign? Was it a business expansion? More to the point: Did you go out of business because of that change, or did you grow?

I'll bet you grew. Business owners tend to hold on to faulty beliefs about what they can and cannot do because they are once bitten, twice shy. The pain of past failures is so traumatic that instead of analyzing why they failed and ensuring they don't repeat the mistake, they decide not to try again at all.

When this happens, anxiety conditions the business owner to believe that success is out of reach. Fear disables, even paralyzes, them from embracing an idea that could move them toward their goals.

How many goals have you set based on what you believed was realistic? How many times have you stopped yourself from trying something because you believed you couldn't do it?

When my first company was sold out from under my feet, my professional and financial life derailed my goals and ambitions, and I lost my positive perspective. I threw a never-ending pity party and griped and complained. This went on for a long time. Every morning I dragged myself out of bed feeling like a washed-up has-been.

However, I was fortunate to have great mentors and friends whom I could trust to speak the truth to me—and speak it they did, in the form of a consistent message: *Refocus your thoughts away from what went wrong in your last business and focus on what you could do right in your next one.* As you know, my mentor and friend Hector LaMarque finally said to me, "What has been done in the past is nothing more than an opportunity to perfect what you are going to do in the future. That's it—nothing more, nothing less."

So move on. Just decide what it is you want to do, and do it!

Through the help of mentors like Hector and the great authors I'd read, I rediscovered the motivation and focus necessary to start not one, but two new companies with the intention of starting many more. There were many people who told me I could never accomplish what I ended up accomplishing during that time. In just ten years, Audigy was generating in excess of $40 million, received awards six straight years from the *Oregon Business Journal* as the number one fastest-growing private company on the West Coast, and won five *Inc. Magazine* 500 awards, three top workplace awards, two entrepreneur-of-the-year awards for me, and many other accolades.

This is a true testament to just how wrong all the naysayers in my life had been who refused to believe anything is possible if you commit to believing in it. Decide what you want to do and simply do it. And, as Grant Cardone says, "Might as well 10X it!"

Think of those old limiting beliefs as pieces of coal you've been carrying around because you've grown more comfortable with your limitations than you'd care to admit. You're clutching them out of desperation, thinking that someday you may need them to build a fire and get warm. But that's just your faulty perception twisting the truth. In reality, you're perfectly warm already. The fire has never completely gone out; it simply needs to be reignited. Have the courage to reignite that fire and watch your life transform.

I have found that the single best way to break through old and outworn beliefs is to adopt a learning mindset, one open to new ideas and practices, even—and especially—when they are not your own. You have to make your desire to *change* stronger than your desire to be right. If you haven't reached your stated goals and objectives after a period of working toward them, you either aren't being honest with yourself about what you really want, or you are allowing your beliefs to get in your way. If you're unwilling to challenge your beliefs in order to achieve your goals, it tells everyone, especially your staff, that *you are the problem.*

When I sit down with business owners, they often tell me that their staff members are all on the same page and are implementing changes. But when I interview the employees, I hear a different story. Not only are they not on the same page, the supposed changes aren't being implemented either. I have to return to the owner and gently say, "You're going in one direction, and everyone else in your organization is headed in another." Almost without fail, those businesses end up with no changes and no growth. I know this for a fact, since many of those same owners have come back to me one or two years later, reporting no positive movement.

It isn't a question of moving from negative thinking to positive thinking. It's a matter of moving toward right thinking. Every decision you make and every action you take is based on your level of awareness of the truth at that moment. In order to be successful, you must constantly work to change and expand your level of awareness. You may believe that your market doesn't have enough room to grow, but your competition is three times your size and growing at 30 percent per year. In that case, your belief that there's no room to grow is based on ceding that 30 percent to your competition.

Why would you automatically default to this belief in your limits? Right-thinking people never accept such limits as their fate. They reject them by saying, "There seems to be an increase in competition. What can we do that we haven't thought of yet to win a greater share of our market?"

MODELING YOUR BELIEFS TO YOUR TEAM

A company culture is really the sum of how you and your team members think, believe, and behave. Culture also reflects the collective self-image of your team. As a leader of others, you are responsible for helping each member of your staff develop a self-image that is in alignment with what you are asking them to accomplish.

In the companies I have built over the years, I have given the books that we use in our team training sessions to every new employee. These are the same books we offer to the clients we advise and manage. Each of these books communicates a principle by which our company operates. We want our employees to think of themselves as a bigger part of our company, not as mules collecting paychecks. We do this because we value our employees and want them to have a self-image that communicates value. If they don't believe we value them, and they don't value themselves, our customers certainly won't feel valued.

Beyond Positive Thinking: A No-Nonsense Formula for Getting the Results You Want by Robert Anthony is another book that we use to help our employees and clients think in terms of solutions rather than problems. Once in a while, an employee or client comes to me to discuss something that might be going wrong in the company. My first question is always, "What do you think we can do about this?" We train our employees to think of themselves as problem-solvers, which lifts their self-image because they then see themselves as part of our company's winning strategy. Imagine what it would be like to hire people with this kind of winning self-image!

The best time to start doing this is when you're hiring. Here is a sampling of questions you can ask prospective employees to determine their self-confidence and self-esteem level:

How would you define self-confidence?

How self-confident do you believe you are?

Tell me about a situation that might demonstrate your confidence to do this job.

Walk me through your process for making a business decision on your own.

What do you think is the difference between confidence and arrogance?

By asking these questions, you are poking your finger into this candidate's confidence, so watch the applicant's body language for signs of uncertainty. If the applicant lacks self-confidence, hire at your own risk.

Remember, you set the tone for the self-image of your organization. If you want to hire self-confident people who like a challenge because they feel they can win, you must believe in yourself and know that you are worthy and competent. Every single employee needs to understand that it is a privilege to get to work with you, since you want to help them succeed and accomplish their personal, professional, and financial goals—and your time and energy are valuable.

Unless *you* feel that way, however, why should they?

INCREASING YOUR LEVEL OF EXPECTANCY

Whether you're the head of a small start-up or a Fortune 500 company, you have a subconscious picture of the revenue size of your business, the number of employees you should have, the income you desire, the type of people you want to work with, the kinds of situations in which you feel comfortable, etc. We'll call this your *environment*. When you begin to feel nervous, you will have the natural inclination to "get back where you belong," luring you to return to the environment that you can relate to most in keeping with your self-image. Whenever you return "back where you belong," you inhibit your growth.

Every time you find yourself in an unfamiliar environment, job, or social situation, it's natural to come up with logical reasons why you shouldn't participate, or why it won't work. The problem is that none of us *deliberately* programmed the kind of environments in which we feel comfortable. Our subconscious minds just absorbed this information through habit. The key to expanding your comfort zone is visualizing yourself in different situations, jobs, relationships, or business settings.

Here's an example. Let's say you train your front office staff to follow up with a potential client. Your staff expresses discomfort with this task because they're afraid clients will feel like they're bugging them or "selling" them. At all my management companies, we built scorecards which show that potential customers give higher customer service scores to businesses that follow up with them. So how do you help your staff work through their faulty beliefs? You educate them about the scorecard process and the importance of follow-up in customer relations. Then, you teach them the skill set necessary to effectively do the job without feeling embarrassed. This can only be done by teaching and developing them to learn exactly how to do it. It requires daily training and commitment from your organization to ensure that everyone on the team is operating at their highest level of contribution.

CHANGE IS YOUR FRIEND, NOT YOUR ENEMY

If our beliefs so often cause us pain and suffering, why don't we change them? Why don't we do what needs to be done to have exactly the kind of life we want? It is because we've been programmed to fear change. We are addicted to certainty. We would rather be certain we are miserable than risk being happy and satisfied. The way to overcome this natural inclination is to separate out the substantive element involved in decisions from the fear factor of dealing with the unknown. When you do so, you may find that it's fear rather than substantive data preventing change.

A big difference between successful people and unsuccessful people is how they handle change and uncertain times. Successful people have anxiety, too, but they don't allow it to immobilize them. They have the tools to honor and work through it. Unsuccessful people let their anxiety stop them in their tracks. This is why so many people in sales can't seem to break through to the next level. Their anxiety doesn't allow them to see the big picture and dream big enough to challenge themselves.

Successful people channel their anxiety into creativity and action. To change your mindset, begin to look at change as a friend instead of as an enemy. Take it with you and allow it to work for you instead of against you. Each one of us is climbing the ladder of life. And each rung on that ladder has new opportunities and new obstacles.

YOUR DOMINANT BELIEFS CREATE YOUR ATTITUDE TOWARD SUCCESS

Attitudes are simply manifestations of your dominant beliefs. Think of attitudes as neither positive nor negative in themselves, but as limiting or liberating, depending on your goals. For example, if you consider yourself to be awkward in social settings, you may be a wallflower at the company party and forgo every opportunity to build new relationships. If you don't think you have any good ideas, you may have a tendency to avoid any situation in which you might be called upon to share them. Since most of your attitudes were developed unconsciously, you need to check them regularly to make sure they aren't standing in your way. For example, if you have a goal you have been unable to attain, ask yourself whether you have an attitude that causes you to avoid situations that would help you to attain your goal. Perhaps you have been reluctant to speak as forcefully as you'd like during meetings or to extend yourself more at parties or other gatherings where you can meet the people you want to meet. Knowing this, make a conscious decision to introduce yourself to someone at a party or speak up—at least *once*—at the next meeting.

As a leader, you need to apply the same resolve with your staff. Regular staff interviews give you the opportunity to learn what your employees are thinking and to assess their attitudes toward the contributions you expect them to make. If you sense that alignment is lacking, you can tweak as needed. At the companies I have created, we have worked hard to implement a constructive employee assessment system. In this assessment, we seek to understand each employee's personal, professional, and financial goals and how they might align with the objectives of our company.

The purpose of this assessment is twofold: to make sure that the employee is in line with the company's goals and objectives, and to make sure that the employee believes that our company is the place where their personal, professional, and financial goals can be achieved. You must weave your employees' personal goals into your overall company objectives, which is exactly what this questionnaire will help you accomplish.

Attitudes either allow us to grow or prevent us from growing—depending on how we use them. It's very important for a business owner to be in tune with each team member's attitudes, to know what situations they are avoiding, and to recognize how those situations can negatively affect their ability to perform their job responsibilities. This is also why it's so important for you and your staff to talk about and focus on as many success stories as possible.

Always over-promote your team's breakthroughs. These stories become new reference points that will help your staff replace negative beliefs with positive ones. Training and celebrating your staff using positive reinforcement programs will prepare them for success.

SURROUND YOURSELF WITH "CAN-DO" PEOPLE

More than half of the business owners I have met have unconsciously conceded the cultural mindset of their organization to a dominant staff member. This is very dangerous in cases where there is negativity in the business. When a dominant staff member emerges, that person is often the most negative individual in the organization, and the self-declared leader influences the organization more than the business owner, clearly working against the owner's and their team's personal, professional, and financial goals. Typically, the business owner doubts it is happening until he or she reads transcripts of the interviews my company conducts with their employees. Only then does the negative influence of the dominant staff member become clear.

Most business owners I've worked with as a coach and consultant started their companies by seeing an opportunity and mustering the courage to go out and take advantage of that opportunity. Then they surrounded themselves with employees who never had the courage or instinct to do the same. They listened to these employees about what could and couldn't be done, and they made decisions based on these faulty beliefs. Many times, business owners stopped thinking for themselves and turned over too many decisions to their employees.

Over time, those business owners became frustrated with their inability to get to the next level and reach their goals. They began blaming those around them. But they were only partly right in doing so: the real problem lay with themselves for expecting too little from their own leadership and from their staff. Remember the Gallup poll I cited earlier showing the prevalence of disengagement and even outright sabotage among US workers? The best way for business leaders to beat the statistics and keep their team engaged is by keeping their thoughts and actions consistent with their objectives and communicating them regularly. This is so important to achieving overall success, and it explains why everyone on your team must be a "can-do" person.

If you're mired in the mindset of, "You can't find good talent—creative, forward-thinking people just don't exist," think again. Like attracts like. If you put a positive attitude out into the universe, people with the same positive attitude are going to be attracted to you. Those people will want to work for you and align their goals with the goals of your business. In other words: *if you build it, they will come.*

But only if you follow the algorithm of the law of intention, the law of action, and the law of attraction. When I was running a sales team, I would have my salespeople make fifty calls a day after they'd done their training. What they didn't know was I already had two or three clients "seeded" and basically teed up to buy each day. So by the end of the week, the new salesperson would make their 250 calls and get five or eight deals. As a result, they would come to work and believe they could continue to get two or three deals a day. I found that once I did that, I never had to push them that much more, because they would feel like they had figured out success.

This example illustrates a broader principle: as a leader your job is to make other people's success easy.

Belief creates outcomes. If you practice the principles in this book on a daily basis, they will allow you to be bigger than your belief system. Then you will produce results that will give you a new belief system, which will allow you to grow even more. Living with fear and doubt is like driving with the emergency brake on. Once you release the brakes, the joys of creating are yours for the taking.

And the freedom to create your life is the most potent game-changer of all.

For additional resources, get immediate access to exclusive behind the scenes videos that uncover even more items I couldn't share in this book. To access these exclusive resources, visit NineFigureTools.com

RH Shipping Lifts Its Belief Lid

Rudolf Hess, Founder

The COVID pandemic was probably the greatest thing that ever happened to me. It was a tragedy for the world, but it forced me to do something I had neglected to do for far too long: reacquaint myself with my family.

Born into a shipping family in Mexico, I ventured into a new challenge twenty seven years ago when I established RH Shipping, a worldwide air, ocean and land cargo transportation company. Our specialty is to ship anything of any size anywhere in the world, and to do so faster than anyone else. We'll ship something as small as a car battery and as large as a 1,000-metric-ton piece of heavy machinery. It hardly needs saying that we travel by land, sea, and sky to deliver for our customers. We cover all the logistics that guarantee a door-to-door delivery, even if we have to pick up a part, put it in a briefcase, and deliver it by hand.

The shipping business depends so much on so many factors that it is constantly going up and down. Through the ups and downs, however, I was doing well until the global crisis of 2008 crippled the economy. For the next year, business dropped 50 percent, although by 2010 we had begun to climb back out from the crisis. That was the year I moved my family to Houston, away from a place that had been our home but had grown violent because of the gangs. When someone was shot within five hundred feet of our home, I knew it was time to go. So I opened an office in Houston and for the next decade, I was all about sell, sell, sell, sell—even though we had no defined sales strategy.

I was constantly on the go between my office in Houston and our Mexican offices. When I was home in Houston, I fell into bed exhausted, of absolutely no use to my family. I lost some of the most important years of my children's lives as I traveled back and forth between the US and Mexico. I missed my child's first lost tooth and first cold. We were making money, but not growing. I felt stuck. My mother came to visit me in 2020 and I told her I didn't think I could keep going. But I felt I had, because I had a hundred people who worked for me and depended on me.

COVID hurt the shipping industry but gave me a measure of freedom just to have time to think and be with my family. Before COVID, I had stopped exercising completely; when the pandemic hit, I started exercising regularly and feeling healthier and fitter. I lost twenty pounds! I began reading books, which recharged me mentally. Reading changed my life and made me want to prepare for the time when the economy would open up again. When it did, I realized I needed a growth strategy that would allow me to keep competing—in what was, after all, a global business that required travel—but also to have a personal life. I found that strategic growth mindset with Brandon Dawson and Grant Cardone.

The first thing I learned from Brandon and Grant was that it was okay to want to make more money, as long as making the money made you happy and not miserable and allowed you to achieve your goals. Money didn't make you happy all by itself—I knew that—but it helped you to be happy. I embraced this philosophy and taught my employees to embrace it as well.

The second thing I learned was that I didn't—and couldn't—do so much just by myself. If we were to grow, we had to train more leaders within our business who could take what I taught them and teach others. Everyone in my company set their sights higher. Thanks to the 10X 360 philosophy of Grant and Brandon, we set a goal of becoming a $1 billion company in ten years. I told my team that if the company achieved its goals, each of them would achieve their goals as well. This has created some very exciting and challenging times at RH Shipping.

For example, we made a commitment never again to sell price, even when it costs us a project. We sell our service, which is based on our global network of shippers and attention to every detail, right up to the point when our client receives delivery of the shipment. That may sound like we're just doing our job—delivering what we promise to deliver—but many shippers, even those much larger than us, do not consistently achieve this. One client we initially lost to a large competitor due to the issue of pricing had to pay an extra premium to receive delivery. Selling price undercuts your reputation in the marketplace; just as bad, it also undercuts your own belief in what you can accomplish because once you've begun accepting less, you will quickly get out of the habit of expecting more. We don't just throw our salespeople out there and say, "Sell more!" We constantly give them additional training opportunities with Brandon and Grant's team.

We've also begun doubling down on sales meetings. On a typical day, we'll have a meeting in the morning and another one in the afternoon. We have taught our team to use the meetings not to sit and listen or just report out, but to actively seek help when they run into challenges. The help can come from a manager, or it can come from a colleague in sales. Sometimes one of the managers will decide that it makes sense to jump on a call with the salesperson and the client. This has made us more of a team, and even though each person has his or her own individual goals, they are focused on the company's goals as well. As a result of investing in our employees and working differently, we are closing on the sale of more accounts than we have ever done before.

Before meeting with Brandon, I had been stuck for years, doing $38 million of revenue with declining profitability every year and concern about the future. Once I made the decision to take action, meet Brandon and his team, and adopt his mindset to business, I took my business from $38 million to $92 million two years later.

Another result of working with Brandon has been investing more in the future and living less day-to-day. When you work hard, it can be tempting to play maybe a bit too hard and live beyond your means. This was a problem for me, I admit. But I have become more disciplined and find great satisfaction in taking care of my people and seeing them come out of their comfort zones and invest in their futures. They are buying homes and sending their kids to college. So much of what we have been able to accomplish comes down to raising the ceiling on our belief in what is possible.

CHAPTER 12

Make Your Business Work for You

Through the years, there have been roughly two types of business owners with whom my experience has brought me into close contact, and often close relationships. One is the businessperson who works for his or her business; the other is the businessperson whose business works for *him or her*. I teach that every business owner should demand that their business work for them for the purpose of providing the life they want and the opportunity for their team to succeed. The job of a business is to create resources, opportunities, and results. Make it your mission to force your business to comply with these three areas.

There is a huge gap between these two types of business owners, and if I could wish anything for you from reading this book, it is that you transform yourself from a business owner who is enslaved to your business to a business leader who makes your business do its job for you, your team, and the mission of the organization.

First, know that there is a reason you created your business or are seriously thinking of doing so. You wanted to turn your ideas into inspired action and felt you had the vision, commitment, and execution mindset needed in order to be successful. This is where the entrepreneur separates himself or herself from everyone else. Second, know that your employees generally won't have all three of these characteristics ingrained in them; this is where genuine leadership is needed. Author and business administration professor Warren G. Bennis said, "Leadership is the capacity to translate vision into reality." When we work with businesses, the one consistent element that gets lost is the vision or big picture that provides the compass for everyone to follow.

It's easy for employees to lose sight of why they need to execute and stay committed to the big picture, so, as the business owner, you must never stop articulating your vision and how their responsibilities directly affect the realization of that vision. You must always be selling the big picture and inspiring your employees toward the goal. This is why I call it inspired action. Once everyone understands where the company is going, they must be individually and collectively committed to the goals of the organization, and they must understand their duties and job functions, as well as how it all ties together. Once that is all in place, everyone must be in execution mode. The only way to bind your team to this vision is to align their personal, professional, and financial goals so that when they win, the business wins.

The bond that links your vision to focused execution by your employees is their commitment. This commitment only comes from a direct understanding of *what is in it for them* personally, professionally, and financially through the business. They need to understand that when the business achieves its goals, they achieve their goals. And you need to understand that when your business achieves its goals, your team achieves theirs. That is the co-investment in growing the business.

This doesn't mean that your employees are selfish; it means that they are human. You need to inspire your team by clearly explaining how their execution of your strategic plan will determine both their success and the company's. This is why the title of this chapter is a bit misleading. It may invite suspicion of a selfish motive or a need to exercise authority. Neither of these interpretations are accurate, as we'll soon demonstrate.

My teams have interviewed thousands and thousands of employees over the years, men and women from a broad spectrum of businesses—Fortune 500 companies, midsized organizations, and small start-ups. Our first question has always been, "Has anyone in this company ever asked you what you want to achieve personally, professionally, and financially through your employment here?" Ninety-five percent of the time, the employees say no. If your employees don't think that you care enough to know what they want, why should they care about what you want? Contrast this to fully understanding what your employees want to accomplish and helping them to succeed. Do you think they would care more about what you want and what the business needs to succeed if they knew you cared about them?

Successful employee engagement involves five levels of expertise. Level one is finding great people. Level two requires that you present a compelling case for why they would want to join your team. Level three requires that you design and align their success within the organization. In level four, you need to develop them so they can grow and scale personally and help the business grow and scale. Finally, the fifth level requires you to have programs in place to retain them. To build and scale a successful team within your organization over the long run, you must find, attract, align, develop, and retain.

In my experience, business owners suffer from what I call "entrepreneurial dilemma," a condition where they don't recognize that most employees are not entrepreneurs. The majority of employees want to be developed, want job security, and want to be shown how to accomplish their work successfully. So the more you can set your employees up for success—from the moment you interview them, to when you make a job offer, to their 30-, 60-, and 90-day onboarding plan—the better quality of candidate you'll be able to bring on.

The problem is that entrepreneurs have a blind spot when it comes to non-entrepreneurs. I assume that you became a business owner because you hated having a boss tell you what to do all the time. You hated having to be told when to come to work, what to say, how much you got paid, how fast you were promoted, what type of clothes to wear, when you could take vacation, etc. Eventually, you struck out on your own. Through that experience, whether or not you enjoyed immediate success (and even if you failed), you realized that you could never work for someone else again—and would almost certainly be fired within ninety days should you try to do so.

I know many entrepreneurs who view themselves as essentially unemployable. My own experiences validated this when my company was sold. It's extremely rare to find an ex-owner who will work for someone else with the same dedication as they did when they owned their own business. It's contradictory to their core beliefs, even if the reason they sold their business was to eliminate getting bogged down with all of the responsibilities of business ownership.

So why can't you turn an entrepreneur into an employee? It has to do with their self-image (a self-image I have no problem with). How do you build a company with people who aren't like you—people you can't identify with and subconsciously don't relate to as well as you do to other entrepreneurs? If you're dependent on people you can't understand or relate to, how can you build your business around them? This is the entrepreneurial dilemma.

I believe that the single biggest limiting factor in an entrepreneur's ability to grow a business is the lack of development of employees. Why? The business owner tends to treat employees the same way he or she wants to be treated—by being left alone. If you hear yourself repeat any of the following beliefs, either aloud or silently, you can be sure that you are falling prey to the entrepreneurial dilemma in which you see yourself as a kind of reluctant superhero:

- "I have to do everything myself!"
- "No one works as hard as me!"

- "I'm the only one who can do it!"
- "I don't trust anyone else, so I have to do it myself!"
- "I wish I could find good help!"
- "People are just too lazy!"
- "I can't trust people to follow through!"
- "No one cares like I do!"
- "I tried to turn that responsibility over, and they screwed it up!"

The exclamation points indicate that these aren't rational thoughts so much as outbursts of emotion that hide the truth. This may be a hard pill to swallow, but the truth is if you haven't found good help, it isn't because it doesn't exist—it's because you have been unable to attract the right types of people into your life because of the way *you* are. Even if you attract them, they'll eventually leave if you ignore them and don't help them to develop. This is why Gallup poll numbers are consistent every single year when they show that out of 100 million US workers, two-thirds admit that they're disengaged, while some admit to actually sabotaging their place of business.

The best an owner can do to keep 60–70 percent of their team engaged is to paint a huge picture of success, showing employees how they can win personally, professionally, and financially inside that picture.

HELPING OTHERS ACHIEVE SUCCESS IS YOUR KEY TO FREEDOM

As I worked on growing my own business in the early days, I came to the realization that I had been trying to motivate all the people around me to do their jobs so that I could get what I wanted, not taking into consideration what they wanted (individually or collectively) out of the experience of working with me. Essentially, I pushed everyone uphill so that I could achieve success for myself. That wasn't leadership; it was sheepherding, cattle driving, or some other unflattering metaphor. Small wonder, indeed, that I used to go home every night muttering to myself stuff like, "If you want it done right, Brandon, I guess you have to do it yourself."

That was what I believed at the time.

What I've learned in the years since is that by recruiting others and then listening to their wants and desires, I am able to inspire and lead them to personal, professional, and financial success. I strive to approach everything with an intense and competitive mentality but in a gentle, nurturing, nonintimidating way. What does this translate to? In my conversations with the people who work for and with me, I don't accept excuses, but I can be totally relied upon to focus on solutions. It means that every conversation provides an opportunity to help my employees learn and grow.

If I'm dedicated to helping others, it follows that it's my job to help them discover why what they're saying and doing isn't getting the results they want. Of course, if they aren't getting the results they want, it means I'm not getting the results I want, either. And the business isn't getting the results it needs to succeed and do its job of providing resources and opportunities for everyone who's contributing to building it.

If I'm not building my employees up and helping them make better decisions so they can work more independently, as the entrepreneur I'm stuck doing everything myself. When I was just starting out, the biggest problem in my company was that we didn't duplicate knowledge and know-how and teach it down the line. We had to search for an expert at the last minute and try to keep them happy or settle for less than we needed because no one was trained for the challenge at hand. But leadership isn't about plugging holes with expensive one-offs; I wanted my leadership to include the freedom to concentrate on developing others.

So I created a four-step process that I now keep in mind when it comes to my relationship with others in my business.

1. Perfect processes for duplication.
2. Teach others to duplicate best practices.
3. Lead by nurturing and teaching self-accountability and results-driven activities.
4. Make sure I have a business model that aligns everyone's interests based on targets attained.

You may recall this process at work in the chapter on starting my company Audigy, when I trained my first hire, Mason Walker, to make sales calls to prospective clients in an industry about which he knew practically nothing. By mastering a technique that I had perfected to engage customers' deeper needs and concerns, regardless of what we were selling, Mason was able to help Audigy grow faster than even I anticipated.

LET YOUR COMPANY WORK FOR YOU

There's no point to working if you don't have the time and money to enjoy the people you love. When I set out to build one of my management companies, Audigy, it was my intention from the beginning to build a successful company that would not inhibit my ability to live the life I wanted.

I set it up so that I immediately began training others to do tasks rather than simply saying, "Here, let me do it. It'll save time." I made it a priority to find people who could take over the tasks on my dreaded list so that I could spend my time being more creative and productive. You can do the same, taking care to achieve a win-win by handing off tasks that are on the other person's joy list.

If you want to change your business to one that can function without you working day in, day out, you have to recognize that you, as the business leader, must change from the inside out. You have to flip the switch on your old belief—again, rooted in your self-image—that you are a superhero who has to do it all because, hey, there are just some amazing talents you can't teach, right?

Wrong.

At least, it's wrong if you want to have any kind of life. This is why it's often hard for business owners to make the jump from business ownership to freedom from their businesses. The thought process required to move from owning and working in your own company to having your company work for you is a complete switch. The truth is, if you became a business owner out of the desire to *not* be an employee, you may *unconsciously* hold a fairly low opinion of most employees. And if this is the case, that is exactly who you will attract to your business: less than capable or trustworthy employees.

The far better and more advantageous route would be to expect the best out of the people you welcome into your employ and then ensure you are leading in a way that will help them meet these expectations. Instead of asking yourself (with a whine), "Where have all the smart people gone?" ask yourself:

"How can I change so that I attract dependable people?"

"What do I offer that makes people want to work with me?"

"What am I offering as mentorship to others?"

"How do I get others to trust me so that I can trust them in return?"

"How do I develop others?"

"How do I learn to train others so that they, too, can have success through my business?"

"How can I better develop my skills so that I can help my employees develop theirs?"

"How can I develop a core leadership group that will repeat this throughout the organization?"

What do all of these questions have in common? The word *I*. In this case, the focus is on you, not on them. This is because you're taking responsibility for how the buck stops with the leader.

Remember that the attributes that make you a great entrepreneur are not the same attributes that make you a great manager or leader. Your appetite for risk-taking and your never-say-never mentality may have inspired you to become a business owner. But not everyone is like you, so when you give your employees their task with a sink-or-swim mentality, they're just as likely to sink as they are to swim, which, in turn, reinforces your belief that you can't find any "good people."

Break out of this vicious cycle by hiring a person with a good attitude and a capable skill set, and focus on inspiring them to identify their own personal, professional, and financial goals. Show them how you will train and develop them in a way that will guarantee success. Explain to them that failure is not an option in the fight toward achieving their goals, and that you are going to make all the necessary investments to help them succeed. Of course, if their goals are divergent from your own, they may need to work elsewhere, but most people want to grow, learn, and conquer challenges. You can absolutely help your employees to do that.

When I have these conversations with my own team, I always make an extra point of offering the following pep talk, which is also a brutally honest statement of expectation:

> As long as I see you investing in yourself, I will invest along with you. If I see you aren't investing in yourself through personal growth, the question you have to ask yourself is, why would I invest in you? If we aren't investing in each other, we aren't growing, and I refuse to not grow. If you don't invest in your success, then you're certainly not going to be interested in investing in the success of the organization or your other team members.
>
> Since I'm totally dedicated to assisting you in your growth, I have an expectation that your personal growth is something you're going to take seriously. If I see that this is not a focus and commitment on your part, our relationship at the company will be over, since I refuse to invest in people who won't invest in themselves or on behalf of the rest of the team. Are we on the same page?

This conversation is held during each potential employee's very *first* interview. I set my expectations very high so that each candidate knows exactly what I'm looking for.

Make the development of your staff and their success your number one priority. Just be smart enough to ensure that their success is consistent with the needs and priorities of your business. The more you have this conversation with your team, the more your team will have the confidence to do things for themselves, and the less you will eventually need to do for them yourself. But remember, it's your belief that limits you, not other people.

THE POWER OF POSITIVE PERSUASION

The key to leading is to persuade others to believe that they are far more capable than they think they are and to get them to stop dwelling on or reinforcing their own limitations. You want your employees to begin focusing their attention on where they want to go or what they want to become. As the leader, it is your responsibility to help them chart their course and understand how to accomplish it through their employment with you. And if this eventually leads a key employee toward a goal outside your doors, don't try to hold on to him or her out of fear. Let this employee go with your blessing and with the confidence that you can attract someone else to fill their shoes.

In order to get help and cooperation from others in reaching a goal, your biggest challenge will be getting others to believe in you. And the best way I know to do this is to make it about them, not about you and your business. Whether I am working with my own team or with clients, my responsibility is to help others change their level of expectation and inspire them to believe and take direct action to drive results at high impact. This is something you can also do by inspiring your own belief and activating your own passion. And how do you do that? Through evaluating your own self-image, checking your limiting beliefs, practicing positive self-talk, and visualizing the results you want and then writing them down.

This will ultimately be some of the best advice I give you in this book: teach yourself and others how to set targets, take massive action, and create the desired life you collectively want through your business.

WHEN YOU HELP OTHERS, YOU HELP YOURSELF

One of the most limiting factors in the majority of companies is that they have no mechanism to align everyone's interests with that of the business. The reason for this is that the relationships are built strictly around economics. When everything is transactional, it becomes nearly impossible for others to think they have real skin in the game, at least not any more than is required to get their next paycheck or bonus. When everything is transactional, there is nothing bigger than themselves to inspire allegiance and dedication beyond money.

When building your business, consider the advantage of building it not for you but for *them*—for your team and the clients you serve. I've built businesses for myself to prove I could, and I've built businesses to help others succeed in their lives. Guess which ones were more successful and fun to lead? Even after the sale of Audigy, the company continued to be wildly successful. There were no losers with the business model I built, which was certainly not the traditional *I take from you in order to make money* business model. This was the *I will help you in order for both of us to make money and support and help each other achieve our goals and have the lives we want* model.

In other words, my businesses are all absolutely aligned with my core values. Is yours?

As we practice these principles, we not only help ourselves, but through our example, we also empower others to live their best lives by our example. Our contribution—the sharing of our time, our talents, and our resources—is essential in creating wealth and business success. The more you give to others, the more you receive in return. So you must give the very thing that you want the most. If you want money, give money. If you want love, give love. If you want recognition, give recognition. If you want respect, give respect. In this respect, you not only get *when* you give, you also get *what* you give. Remember, output amplifies input: the more you put out, the more you receive.

You must also acknowledge the abundance that you have already and allow it to overflow to others. When you do this, your awareness of your abundance increases. As your awareness increases, your abundance will also increase. This abundance isn't necessarily monetary, however. It may be knowledge, ability, passion, or insight. Ultimately, it's the overall impact that you've created from your stated objective.

Because I follow these principles, I am surrounded by loyal, hard-working, and appreciative employees in my companies. They demonstrate through their performance that they take the time I spend with them very seriously. This ultimately makes my life much easier, and I'm not at all trapped or confined by my business. They understand that my job is to help them accomplish their stated goals and objectives, and their job is to demonstrate that they are willing to invest in themselves in order to make them happen. Together, we spur one another onward toward success. That's what it means to have your business work for you.

One final note: if you can't find a way to get your people to work for the business, you will never, ever, get your business to work for you.

For additional resources, get immediate access to exclusive behind the scenes videos that uncover even more items I couldn't share in this book. To access these exclusive resources, visit NineFigureTools.com

CASE STORY

10X Health Systems Rekindles the Passion

Gary Brecka, Co-Founder

Much of the time, people who write about entrepreneur-ial successes focus on the end result of success. They overlook the backstories: the stress of trying to make payroll by dipping into their personal bank accounts, and trying to hire people and grow their businesses while making sure everything is operating well and accounts payable and receivable are rolling along. Don't get me wrong; I wouldn't trade the journey we've taken for the world, but the whole story needs to be told, if only because it's more interesting.

I spent years working in the mortality industry for a life insurance company. My job was to sift through years' worth of medical records and predict, to the year and month, how long a prospective policy-holder was likely to live. Then I'd send the information to the policy-writing team. The most interesting part of the work was the insight I gained into what made people live longer or shorter due to variations in their lifestyle and genetic influences. I thought it would be excit-ing to work on the other side of the business and focus on vitality and helping people, so in 2017, with my fiancée, Sage Workinger, we started a company called Streamline Medical Group.

The business used blood testing and genetic testing to provide an in-depth picture of a person's health and wellness profile, and offered customized IV therapy based on their needs. You may have heard of the term *biohacking*. That's what Streamline did, and we were very good at it, even though we initially struggled to grow our business. We opened up in Naples, Florida, right next to a very busy LA Fitness. We figured there would be a nice, steady flow of wellness-oriented customers we might be able to cherry pick.

Sage and I were new to entrepreneurship, and it didn't take us long to have our first crisis. In 2018, we realized we couldn't keep up payroll for six employees and pay our mortgage on a beautiful 5,500-square-foot house, so we sold our house and lived in a small rental Sage owned in order to make payroll.

For the next couple of years or so, in an effort to expand our business, we went through a series of failed partnerships and joint ventures, including one with a supplement company and another with a wellness franchise. All brought some degree of financial loss for us. Finally, we decided we'd had enough of trying to find partners and were just going to knuckle down and run the business ourselves. At the end of 2020, we met Brandon and started working with him. At the time, our business was doing $150,000 a month.

Like Grant, I met Brandon first as my patient—he enjoyed a successful treatment that enabled him to drop a lot of extra weight and feel better. But his reputation as an expert at scaling businesses preceded him. He was known for being able to fix business operations and show owners how to hire the right people who knew how to help you grow. I was a little skeptical at first, but we met with him and, after learning only the bare bones of our company, Brandon proceeded to tell me, in exact detail, everything that was wrong with it. I was impressed. You would have thought he had already worked with us! He knew exactly what was causing our pain—we were spending way too much time sweating the small details—but he also reassured us by saying we had something special that deserved to be scaled.

And that evenhanded feedback sealed our mentoring relationship.

Working with Brandon, we grew our business to over $500,000 a month. Not long afterward, Cardone Ventures acquired Streamline and changed the name to 10X Health Systems with the hope that we could build into something much bigger. No sooner did we start working with Brandon's team than it became glaringly obvious that we needed to pull back and stop focusing so much on *running* the business that we left no time for *leading* it and our team. Brandon's team conducted a complete audit of our staff and helped us set clear goals and responsibilities for everyone in the company, including Sage and me.

It wasn't easy. For six months, we had daily Zoom meetings during which we built spreadsheets for everything under the sun and began putting incentives, targets, and measurements in place for everyone in the company. But fairly quickly something amazing started to happen: the period of friction between our team and Brandon's team came to a close. We experienced a huge boost in morale as we all began to understand the company in a much deeper way and were able to see progress day-to-day, week-to-week, and month-to-month. Our new customer acquisition was strong to begin with, but Brandon showed us the potential to grow far more, and faster, by paying more attention to our repeat business, which took off.

Sage and I used to rarely have a moment to talk and catch up with each other about work; now, we found we could talk about the business several times a day and make important decisions.

Within a year of selling our Streamline business to Brandon and Grant, we went from making $500,000 a month to over $5 million a month. We grew from six employees to sixty in our five locations in Florida, California, and Arizona. When we first met Brandon, I couldn't have told you very much about our revenues or anything else outside of our core services to our clients, which is the thing I love to do. Now I know every aspect of our business like the back of my hand. One of our key goals is to have a thousand franchises out there under our corporate name. I have to pinch myself when I say this because it was only a little over a year ago that Sage and I swore off partnerships or other kinds of joint ventures because they'd always crashed and burned in the past.

The most important hires we made were the ones that freed Sage and me from the day-to-day operations so we could focus and think through this aggressive expansion. This has been a true game-changer for us in many ways, not least because we now have more time to forge partnerships and be strategic about growing our business. In the past, I would finish an appointment with a client and then proceed to waste an afternoon problem-solving an invoice from a rubber glove vendor. Not anymore. Today, I sit on board of the National Football League Alumni Association Athletica, which is a synergistic organization with ours because we treat many retired football players. I was honored to be invited to speak at the 2022 Pro Football Hall of Fame induction ceremony in Canton, Ohio.

Now that we're part of a bigger team, we have developed our brand's national caché by working with many high-end celebrities, appearing on *The Kardashians* on Hulu and working with Dana White, the president of Ultimate Fighting Championship (UFC). White's physical and mental strength have improved to such a marked degree that he publicly speaks very highly about his 10X Health Systems transition, helping to earn me the nickname "Celebrity Biohacker."

Sage and I were doing well with our old business but had a sense we were stuck. We might have been tempted to just settle for "comfortable," but we're glad we resisted the urge. Life is much more exciting for us today! We're grateful for our good fortune to have reached out to someone who understood business growth far better than ourselves and partnered with a team that values accountability more than any group of people we've ever known.

So I guess our story has the entrepreneurial happy ending after all.

Legacy and Employee Development: TRC Electronics Goes from a Transactional to Transformational Business

Steve Lagomarsino, Owner

I grew up in an entrepreneurial family. My granddad on my mom's side owned a cabinet-making business and in 1982, after he retired, he and my dad started a new company called TRC Electronics. TRC is a business-to-business wholesale manufacturer of power conversion components that are sold to electronics companies. I still vividly recall conversations we had around the dinner table where we talked about business and creating wealth and opportunities for our family and for others. For as long as I can remember, I knew that, one way or another, I was going to be an entrepreneur and a leader.

I've always loved to work. A lot of kids pick up jobs in high school, but how many do you know who worked sixty hours a week? That was me. I worked some at TRC but also at a local sporting goods store. By the time I was a high school senior, I had been promoted to store manager. In college I earned a bachelor's degree in electrical engineering, and in 1998 I took my first job out of college working for my dad. By that time, the company was pulling in around $2 million annually, and the more I learned the ropes, the more I began to form some of my own ideas of where the family firm might go.

My dad's view of TRC's growth potential was more cautious than mine. He'd already accomplished more than he'd ever dreamed of, so he didn't want to risk very much. I was a young kid coming in with nothing to lose and lots to gain. Besides, I thought it was really important that I not put my feet on the desk and ride my dad's coattails. I thought my responsibility was to do my part to take us to the next level.

In the early 2000s, online marketing was new and offered a very inexpensive entry point, so I learned how to create an e-commerce site. My dream was to help us go from being a regional player in the Northeast to a national presence. My dad supported my interest in e-commerce, so I introduced TRC to internet marketing, and by 2010 our annual revenue had grown to around $8 million. During this time I also bought out my granddad and became a minority owner. At this point, even though we were growing, I still felt we were leaving so much untapped potential on the table. I told my dad, "Either I buy you out . . . or I leave."

We got a valuation on the company and I paid full value for it and have run it for the past twelve years.

As the owner of my own business, the first thing I learned was that I was an awful leader. I could sell and market the lights out of our products, and up to a point I could lead by example. I mean, nobody had a greater work ethic than I did. We had about eight people working for TRC and needed to add more to grow, but I didn't just want to add bodies. I wanted TRC to do more for my employees than just give them a paycheck. This was when I wondered, *Is there someone out there who understands purpose and impact as well as profit? Someone who thinks of a company as a place where a leader can bring his staff along— and up—with him? Most importantly, someone who has done it before?*

I had my doubts that such a person existed.

And then, in August of 2019, Grant Cardone introduced me to Brandon Dawson. Brandon and I talked for quite a while, and he invited me to explore how his team could work with us over the long term. I brought four members of my team along—my sales and engineering and accounting leaders—so that whatever there was to learn wouldn't just be in my head. I wanted others to be able to come back from the event with ideas to implement. Over the course of the two days, which included dinner at Brandon's house, Brandon put our little group through some serious soul-searching about what we wanted our business to be about in the present, and also what we wanted to be remembered for—what we wanted our legacy to be.

By the end, I pretty much figured out that I wanted to be remembered for business leadership more than business ownership. I wanted to be known as someone who changed the trajectory of people's lives for the better by helping them develop themselves not just professionally but also personally.

And that is the course I set for myself and for my team. For example, when Anton Gordon, whom we call AJ, came to us thirteen years ago, he didn't own a car. He took a bus to work an entry-level job in our warehouse. AJ wasn't where he wanted to be in life, either in terms of his working life or, quite frankly, the people with whom he associated. I began working with him on his goals and skills, and he has developed himself in every area. He is now a warehouse manager, a homeowner, and an investor—both literally in the financial markets but also in his own future. He has gotten married, and his wife now regularly says to me, "I don't know what you did with this guy, but please keep doing it."

What I did was show AJ that his success in his work—one key metric for success in warehouses involves customer satisfaction and retention—meant making sure we were shipping the right product at the right time, which is what keeps customers happy. Accuracy and overall productivity are easy to measure, but you have to measure them, not just talk about it. AJ never, ever used to read books or improve himself. Now he does. He is enrolled in Cardone Enterprise's Business Mastery Leadership program and constantly seeks to develop himself.

Another member of my team, Lisa Tran, came in as an entry-level bookkeeper and constantly asked us what more she could do. Our answer was, "Plenty." She recently completed her master's and took online courses in human resources to qualify to manage the HR function in our organization. As I became better at communicating with my team, I passed my knowledge of that skill on to Lisa. She's gone from entry-level bookkeeper to senior director of operations. Now she's heading our accounting, purchasing, and HR functions. She has improved her communication and coaching skills to the point where she manages several people. This has not only freed her from some of the routine tasks she used to perform, it has also freed me to do more higher-level planning.

The number one thing that holds people back from being successful is a lack of confidence. People usually think they are far less capable than they really are. They are programmed to fear failure, even though by setting higher goals you can actually succeed even if you fail to reach them because your bar is set so much higher. I've always considered myself a confident person, but even I was short-selling what we were capable of doing with our company. As I began to raise my sights on what we could accomplish, I was able to duplicate this confidence, along with the expectations that came with it, with my team. Through Brandon's mentorship, I realized that when people duplicate their skills and know-how and teach others, they can magnify the effect. Now my team is helping the company and helping the people they are leading.

I knew I was changing the trajectory of their lives when they began to become leaders in other areas of their lives as well as at TRC.

For example, Lisa is working on certifications for becoming a physical trainer for people with health conditions, a subject that is close to her heart. Rather than continue to merely cope with issues, Lisa has been able to visualize herself as someone who can lead herself and others to living healthier lives.

That makes me feel incredibly proud.

Before we began working with Brandon and Cardone Ventures, we had no real company culture. When we started initiating the culture I wanted, we experienced high turnover in the business by people who were not in alignment with us, including some I had *believed* were aligned with us. But with the mentoring I was getting from Brandon, I hung in there and started hiring the kind of people I intentionally wanted to come into the organization. And I started creating the culture I wanted.

When I hear there's no turnover in a company, I know they have a weak culture because there's no way that 100 percent of any company's team members are totally locked in and fully committed to being held accountable in any system. A third of the people are going to be top performers, a third will meet expectations and call it even, and a bottom third will be disengaged; with this last group, an owner needs to either move them up or move them out, voluntarily or involuntarily— more often than not, the moving out happens voluntarily because those people feel uncomfortable as part of a high-performing team.

That is perfectly natural because change *can* be uncomfortable. Even the process of taking goal-setting more seriously can be disquieting to some, and we've had some people self-select out of our organization. We did have some turnover, but if you have no turnover, you clearly don't have accountability. Once you get to the other side of change, it's amazing how much opportunity there really is in the business.

The key was to be transparent about what was needed. One question some members of our team had, especially those not directly generating revenue like sales and marketing, was how to set up metrics to measure their progress toward their goals and the company's goals. My answer was that, one way or another, every position impacts revenue. Our warehouse impacts retention with customers. If we ship the wrong product or fail to work productively, we will lose customers and lose revenues. If we incentivize accuracy in shipping, we all get rewarded.

Let's look at accounting. If we are inaccurate in our billing, it affects our customers' satisfaction levels and we waste time correcting accounting errors. As far as accounts receivable go, not every transaction we process involves credit cards; sometimes we need to chase down unpaid invoices when cash is involved. Revenues don't mean much if companies don't actually collect the money, right? So we have timetables for cash collection. No matter what area of TRC one works in, moving "up" means becoming a top performer in metrics and demonstrating a willingness to become a leader, which means teaching others to perform.

It sounds obvious, but I'd never put it together and documented it and set it in motion.

When I first joined TRC in 1998, all I knew how to do was hunker down and build my business. After spending several years working while being mentored by Brandon and putting structure, process, and leadership in place, I am not only growing my business—I'll do over $50 million in 2023—but I am also doing it remotely from Boca Raton, Florida, where I relocated my family. Because I have built such a remarkable team, I've accomplished so many things. In addition, I've been able to invest with Grant Cardone and Cardone Capital. My passive income from those investments is almost as much as I was paying myself in salary working full-time.

If you told me three years ago my life would look like it does today, I don't know that I would have believed you. Everything in my life has changed because I opened my mind, made different decisions, took action, and focused on becoming a leader versus just purely an operator. Our team has grown to forty-five people. I get to spend more time, especially on weekends, with my family. And I don't have employees asking me to solve building maintenance issues, settle low-impact customer disputes about orders, or deal with employee performance issues when someone is late to work one day!

Coaching my employees to believe more in their abilities and to set more ambitious goals for themselves would have meant little if I had not also worked with them so they could learn how to feel comfortable as problem-solvers. I used to be the only one who really understood how TRC worked, and to an extent I enabled that sort of imbalance.

Now? I have a whole company full of amazing people who want to see how far they can go—and *we* can go. I mean, who wouldn't want to be able to look back at that as their contribution to the US electronics manufacturing industry?

I've had some good mentors in my life, but two stand out above the rest. The first is my dad, who taught me that a leader should always lead by example and never ask others to do something he hasn't or wouldn't be willing to do. In other words, always be an example. And boy, I did just about everything there was to do early on at TRC. Dad also taught me to always be profitable, which might sound pretty basic, but it's one of those things many small businesses have trouble achieving—which is why they go out of business.

My other great mentor is Brandon Dawson, who taught me how to revolutionize my thinking about what my business means to me, which I would characterize as going from transactional thinking to transformational thinking. It's amazing what can happen when you go from setting an example for others to follow to teaching others how to set an example for others to follow.

That's one virtuous circle of business leadership.

CHAPTER 13

The Flow of Abundance

We live in an abundant universe filled with ideas flowing through time and space. It's up to each of us to take what we need from this flow. There is an abundance of ideas that we can use to create more riches in our lives.

If you think about it, *money is an idea in action.* If you stand in the flow of life and say, "There isn't enough," "I can't have," or "I'm not able to," the flow passes right by you. This is also true for your business when you say things like, "I can't afford to grow," "My customers won't pay my prices," "There's no growth opportunity in my market," or "There's too much competition."

According to the law of circulation, the current of life is always flowing, and it's flowing right now. Have you considered that one word for money, *currency,* is related to the word *current? Currency* also means "passing from hand to hand," which suggests that money must be circulated, not hidden, hoarded, or stolen. Those who hoard their money, hide it, or steal it do so from a fear that the world offers a finite amount of anything: money, opportunity, friendship, love . . . you name it. They believe that the key to happiness is to grab their pile and protect it against intruders. This is the essence of the scarcity mindset at work. Everything is about limits.

The problem with this mindset is that it goes *against* the flow of life itself, and the flow of wealth and abundance. When you block circulation through fear (fear of letting go, fear of lack, fear of giving), you stop the flow. That blockage must be removed if you are to experience riches and abundance on a permanent basis.

Abundance is not just about (or even mostly about) money. It is a mindset of confidence and growth of which money is just a part. To illustrate what I mean, consider this fallacy: "If I can just get my hands on a stack of cash, I'll be set for life." Many people think this is true, but it is demonstrably false. As we all know, studies have shown that people who receive large sums of money without working for it, such as through a lottery or inheritance, almost always find themselves back at their original financial level within two years of their windfall. They think they will pay their bills, get out of debt, and start anew if they have the money. But that very seldom happens. More than 90 percent of the people who win large sums of money eventually end up with no more money than they had before their winnings. Their standard of life does not increase and, in many cases, is actually lowered due to excessive spending.

If we divided all the money in the world equally, in a short time the rich would be rich again and the poor would be poor again. Why would this be so? I think it has to do with consciousness. If someone has a consciousness of scarcity, they believe they do not have the skill or power or good fortune to gain wealth. Their windfall from a lottery or inheritance will only change their views on luck, not agency. They will remain unable to expand their wealth, keep it, or replace it.

On the other hand, take all of the money away from a person who has the consciousness of a millionaire with a consciousness of abundance—someone who believes the world offers abundance to all who seek it—and within a short time, he or she will be a millionaire again. Riches start from the mind, not your pocketbook, bank account, or investments. The pocketbook, bank account, and invest-ments are the effects, not the causes, of a mindset of abundance. The cause is always an idea or belief about money. A person is not rich because they have money; they have money because they are already abundant in consciousness.

How would this idea work out in your business?

Take a look at your life and your business and see what's preventing you from keeping your money or having more success. Take a look at where you seem to spend most of your money and your time. Are there other places you'd rather spend them? If so, take a look at what's hold-ing you back. What are your beliefs about circulating money or invest-ing time and energy into your staff's desire to enjoy greater abundance?

MANAGING NEGATIVE BELIEFS ABOUT MONEY

Intentions about money are especially important because many people in our society tend to have a lot of negative beliefs about both money and wealth. For example, do you believe that being rich means you're taking from others or that there isn't enough money to go around? Thinking this way would certainly impose powerful limits on how much money you were willing to accept for yourself and for those on your team. Evaluate your thoughts and beliefs about wealth to deter-mine which ones are holding you back.

In order to clear those limiting beliefs, you must affirm what you want to believe about personal and business wealth. One way to do so is to fill your consciousness with language that empowers you to want more for yourself and your business. Here are some intention statements you might try:

These Are My Affirmations
I choose to build $100 million in net worth.
I choose to be the best father and husband.
I choose to be the best business partner.

I choose to know how to be rich.

I choose to teach my clients and others how to be wealthy.

I choose to deserve material wealth.

I choose to know how to achieve my goals.

I choose to allow my income to exceed my outflow.

I choose to give myself permission to enjoy money and embrace life.

I choose to embrace a life of success and wealth.

I choose to be rich in consciousness.

I choose for my business to have a surplus of cash.

I choose for my business to have cash to invest.

I choose to help my mentors amplify their messages.

I choose to believe that the universe holds unlimited abundance.

I choose to be an example of abundance by creating wealth.

I choose to pay my employees well and to create the best place for people to succeed.

I choose to be the dominant player in my business space.

I choose to profit share and use above-market incentives to surround myself with the best staff.

I choose to teach my team how to become wealthy.

I choose to offer so much value for my customers that they always want to work with me.

I choose to help my clients to build the highest value businesses in their marketplaces.

I choose to help my clients become wealthy.

I choose to offer the best value with the highest returns for my customers.

I choose to offer so much value to my customers that price is never an issue.

I choose to be honest, transparent, and innovative.

I choose to support causes that are important to me and my family.

Note that these intention statements involve others as well as yourself. This is critical because an abundance mindset believes there is an infinite number of opportunities for an infinite number of people; these people will be attracted to each other as colleagues (and as people) because of this shared mindset. Another way to counter the negative and limiting mindset about money involves the concept of a "universal bank." Whenever you give and do not see an immediate return, know that you've made a deposit into the universal bank and that it will return to you with interest at just the perfect moment—often in surprising ways. Whatever you give must come back to you. This is the law of cause and effect, and it cannot be changed.

Don't make the mistake of trying to decide when, and through what channels, your time, money, or good fortune should return to you, but know that if you make a deposit in the universal bank through money or actions, your contributions will return to you in countless ways. Sometimes your abundance will manifest quickly. You may even think it's almost magical. But even if it seems to be slow, know that it's coming right back at you. Karma can be a beautiful thing. Be as confident in this as you are that the sun will rise every morning. Applying this principle as an aspect of the culture of your company will pay huge dividends—not only with your staff, but also with your customers.

Nature shows us how abundance circulates endlessly among those who seek it. A good example is a pond. If water only flows *into* the pond, it will soon stagnate and will no longer support life. If water only flows *out* of the pond, it will soon dry up and will no longer support life. If water flows both into and out of the pond, it will sparkle with purity and support thriving life. You can take a cue from nature's example and apply this principle to your financial circumstances. As you circulate money freely, more money flows into your life.

Another aspect of circulation is release. Start to release everything that is no longer part of what you want to create in your life. Give away material things that you no longer use or want in order to make room for what you *do* want. At least once a year, it's a good idea to go through your home—especially your closet and desk—to downsize by discarding what you no longer use. If you haven't used something in the last twelve months, give it away to friends, employees, or charity.

The act of cleaning out gives you the chance to put what remains in better order, free of the clutter that Ralph Waldo Emerson was referring to when he said, "Beware of holding too much good in your hands." Emerson cautioned against holding on to the present good too tightly out of fear that the future will present no new good. Believing this blocks the flow of new good into your life.

GIVING MUST BE BALANCED WITH RECEIVING

Another important way to increase the flow of abundance in your life is to be a good receiver. Giving must be balanced with receiving. Many people neglect this area of their lives because receiving takes some courage. When you become the receiver, it makes you feel more vulnerable and less in control. When you give, you are in control as the bearer of the "gift," whether it is a compliment or a bonus. Receiving, on the other hand, sometimes makes you feel out of control.

Perhaps you were raised to reject compliments as flattery, or as something that would tempt complacency. Humility is a fine virtue, but don't be so modest that you reject a gift offered to you when you deserve it. Refusing to accept a compliment or bonus not only slights the giver but also affirms that you believe you had nothing to do with your success. Accepting compliments allows the other person to give something to you, and that's important. When you offer a gift, don't you want the other person to receive it with appreciation?

If you look at the whole picture, you have to admit that most of us are, at different times, both giver and receiver. Learning to freely accept what is given to you will help you to become an open channel for wealth. So never refuse anything good that is offered to you. If someone offers you a gift, accept it and say, "Thank you." If you're in a restaurant and someone wants to pay the bill, don't argue.

Just say, "Thank you," and allow them to give to you. Forget about feeling vulnerable or owing something in return. If someone gives you something you don't like or don't need, pass it on to someone else who can use it or enjoy it. There's no shame in regifting when it's done in a spirit of generosity. When you do this, everyone wins. When you refuse a gift someone offers, you not only block the flow of abundance in your life, you also block the flow of abundance in the giver's life.

But remember that when you accept something from someone else, you are also accepting your place in the flow of abundance that comes not only *to* you but *from* you. The more you receive, the more you will have to give. This is an important life lesson but also an important business lesson. Gifts don't have to be big; they can be as simple as listening and supporting an employee who wants to grow. In return, accept their gift of wanting to learn from you.

PLANT "MONEY SEEDS" AND WATCH THEM GROW!

Another way to increase abundance is the process of giving seed money, which is based on the law of circulation. The seed money principle is a sure way to increase the flow of riches into your life. It's about planting seeds of wealth by giving money with the expectation of a tenfold return. In the case of your business, the "seed money" isn't necessarily *actual* money. It can be your time spent developing, mentoring, and coaching your staff.

A farmer can only plant the seeds he has. If he has one hundred seeds, that's all he can plant. To increase his crop, he must plant more seeds than he did the previous season. But he also wants to plant in rich soil that has been given plenty of water and care; otherwise, the field in which the crop was planted would quickly be used up. What is true of planting a crop such as corn also holds true of planting money seeds: Your belief in the person in whom you are investing is the soil. Your expectancy of return is the water that drives the growth.

But in business there is a crucial difference from farming. Consider, for example, a top employee who is becoming burnt-out because he or she is the only one who excels at sales. The best seed you could plant would be the seed of helping that top performer understand the why and how of what they do, and then coaching them to teach others. This can motivate your employee by the prospect of career advancements and, at the same time, provide a new way to train your other staff members for success.

Since beliefs are so important, select a place where you feel your seed money will do the greatest good so that it will multiply. The ideal way to seed your wealth is by contributing to an organization, individual, or activity that you feel will further your personal, professional, and financial growth. And, as I've learned from Grant Cardone, start thinking in terms of 10X returns. You could think of a hundredfold return, but it probably wouldn't be believable in the moment; 10X is much more believable, so start there. And once you accomplish your goals, 10X them again. Do it again and again and again.

▪ ▪ ▪

No matter what you do in your life and in your business, you are going to incur some amount of risk. One of the hardest things to do in life is to take risks. Many people tell me that they're not willing to risk their financial security. They find risk-taking frightening. But here is the truth about risk: everything you do in life involves risk—and that includes doing nothing. Doing nothing involves risk because you will close a door to discovering an opportunity that may never be available to you again. But it takes more than a certain comfort level with risk to succeed; it also takes a belief in your own ability to be successful.

Money and business opportunities exist in the trillions, and many individuals who take advantage of them with dedication and resilience have a great deal of success. Yet others get involved in the same opportunities and never achieve any success. Why would this be? Success or failure with any opportunity depends on aligning your heart and mind with your goals and dreams, which establish your intentions, drive your actions, and are measured by the results you produce. As a business owner, you will quickly learn that when it comes to succeeding, two people within the same company can have the same training, the same compensation, and sell the same thing, but with markedly different success.

It's all about belief, and it all starts with you. When belief is reinforced by massive action that drives results, trust me, you will 10X your belief about what's truly possible.

I invite you to read the story of Pat and Trista Morstad, who experienced the same movement from scarcity to abundance in their company, Precision Landscape and Irrigation. Their self-limiting mindset had left them feeling chronically unsatisfied with their company's profitability, especially given how hard they worked to grow the business from scratch. Through their work with my team, they focused on changing their own mindsets and then their company culture to support what has become an impressive run of growth that exceeded their expectations. (See the Morstads' Case Story at the end of this chapter.)

I realize that scary things can happen financially, but you must go beyond your fear to achieve financial freedom. If you are worried about money, you'll feel powerless to change your financial circumstances. You are not powerless unless you decide you are. All you need to do is change your mindset from one of fear and scarcity to one of courage of abundance and excitedly begin working on taking action toward your stated objectives.

Remember, we are not just talking about hard work here. It's actually harder to work against the natural flow of the universe, which thrives on the constant exchange of resources. I know many hardworking people who never seem to have enough money or enjoy financial freedom. Don't settle for becoming one of them. Open yourself to the flow of wealth that exists in the world; once you've done so and have become a leader of your own destiny, you'll be able to lead others to do the same.

For additional resources, get immediate access to exclusive behind the scenes videos that uncover even more items I couldn't share in this book. To access these exclusive resources, visit NineFigureTools.com

Embracing an Abundance Mindset

Pat Morstad, Precision Landscape and Irrigation, Owner

Our company didn't even have a name for the first six months or so.

When I was out of college, my first career involved working as a golf course superintendent for a company that built high-end courses all over the United States, including a couple of courses for Jack Nicklaus. After I'd done that for a few years, I began developing a small landscaping business as a side hustle. At that time, I had one other guy working with me. We didn't have a name, so we just advertised for landscaping services. We wound up calling it Precision Landscape and Irrigation. Eventually, I found I was making enough money in my side hustle to turn it into my main focus.

I officially filed the paperwork and registered Precision Landscape and Irrigation, LLC, with the State of Minnesota in October of 2009.

We hired some industry consultants who helped us move along and start to be profitable enough for me to take a salary. But I wouldn't say they were necessarily giving us the guidance we felt we needed to take our business to a new level. One might tell us we needed to create "systems," another that we needed to tweak our account ledger, and still another that I needed to stop worrying. But none helped us see the whole picture. None could actually say, "We'll show you how to go from $300,000 in revenues to $5 million—what will happen, and when, and what to look out for and prepare for."

We kind of hobbled along until 2018, by which point we were making $1 million in revenues and netting $80,000–$100,000. We were kind of just stuck in that rut and didn't know how to get beyond that. By then, the business included me; my wife Trista, who did all the books and HR while still working full-time for a local bank; and eight seasonal staff who did the landscaping work—patios, outdoor kitchens, walkways, grading, seeding, irrigation systems, and lawn maintenance . . . you name it. But I was constantly needed in the field to ensure quality results. Our scenario is a little unique from the standpoint of other businesses that are out there. In our business, the season runs from the spring through the early fall, so you basically have 167 days to produce an entire year's worth of money.

One day I was watching *Undercover Billionaire* on the Discovery Channel and trying to see what successful people did to be successful that we weren't doing. Grant Cardone was one of the people featured. He had been given $100, a car, and a tank of gas, and was tasked with building a business valued at $1 million in ninety days. I had heard of Grant before as a well-known sales coach and motivational speaker, so when he ran an advertisement after the program ended, I stayed tuned in. The ad was about the importance of finding mentors who had already done what you want to do and modeling yourself on them. He talked about the importance of mindset in success and said to visit his website if you wanted to learn more.

Within an hour of visiting his website, I heard back from someone in his organization. It turned out that Grant focused on sales, and what I needed were management and operations training, so Grant's staff gave my name to Cardone Ventures, who followed up with a call. Long story short, I paid a substantial fee to attend a two-day course with Grant's partner, Brandon Dawson, and his team. I don't know whether it's the law of attraction that brings you to the right person for the right reason at the right time, but that's instantly how I felt with Brandon. It's hard to explain and hard to understand unless a similar thing has happened to you.

In our first meeting, I tried to absorb a lifetime of business knowledge. It was like trying to drink from a fire hose! I jumped in feet first for a deeper relationship with Brandon's team. The logic of what Brandon was offering and the experience he brought to bear were irrefutable. His team does a deep-dive analysis of your business from a metrics perspective: everything, and I mean everything, about your market, your competition, your employees, your systems (or lack of systems), and your own goals for the business. Then you put together a ten-year plan that has lots of quarterly and annual checkpoints in between to inform you how well you are progressing toward your goals. We spent months working with members of Brandon's team on doing this and came up with a clear path forward. That's now our platform, and it's amazing.

But the most amazing thing of all happened fairly early in our relationship. I was talking one-on-one with Brandon when all of sudden I found myself just kind of spewing out all of the things we had failed to do as an organization in the past—all the missed opportunities and all the windows that had closed on us over the years. Looking back at that moment, I was clearly projecting my lack of confidence and belief in myself and our business. Life offered scarce opportunities, and I felt as though I'd made a career out of missing out on them.

And that's when Brandon said, "You know where this all has to start, don't you? The first thing you have to change is you."

That was a hard pill to swallow, but when someone with Brandon's record of business achievement makes such a comment, it carries weight.

"I could tell the minute we started talking," Brandon told me. "you have become all about what you can't do, what isn't an opportunity, and how everyone else but you seem to understand how the game is played. That's gotta change, right?"

He prescribed two books for me: *Beyond Positive Thinking* by Dr. Robert Anthony and *The 10X Rule: The Only Difference between Success and Failure* by Grant Cardone. After reading the books, I almost immediately began seeing things differently. The world seemed full of opportunity—more than I could possibly take advantage of—and the only thing stopping me from achieving all I wanted to achieve in the world was me. But the key point was that improving my own mindset was only the start; to succeed, those around me would need to adopt the same mindset, one grounded in the belief that everyone has the ability to pursue their dreams and realize them.

Brandon has broken down the whole process of improving yourself and setting goals into three categories: personal, professional, and financial, which he calls your PPF goals. The idea is to decide how you want to change yourself and grow personally, and then begin to work that into the goals of the business in perfect alignment. When you do this for yourself and every member of your team, you create something wonderful, where everyone is working for the same thing. You're all inspired to achieve something and can apply discipline to make sure that you're going in the right direction. Now you're all accountable to each other and can decide whether you are achieving your collective and personal goals.

When you go through PPF goal-setting, you discover that some people can align, while others simply cannot. At our company, achieving alignment took its toll in terms of turnover, and we've had to cycle through a lot of original employees who couldn't adapt to our new goals and bring in new people who fit our new culture. Some self-selected out; others we had to let go. But in all cases, we wished them the very best. There were no hard feelings because we communicated in an open and honest way. When you start to get like-minded individuals who all want to move forward in their lives and be a part of something bigger than themselves, you begin communicating and start working together at a very high level.

With our platform, we have set big goals for our business for the next ten years, including ten thousand new clients, four new locations (for a total of five), and $25 million in revenue.

People ask me what happened to raise my expectations for the business, and I tell them my mindset changed. I'm a person of action but am also cautious to a fault. I always used to ask, "What if this bad thing happened?" or say, "Well, I don't know . . ." Now I've learned to use different language with which to frame an opportunity, such as "that sounds intriguing" or "the worst that can happen is, we'll fail, learn, do better next time, and *still* be ahead of where we'd be if we'd never tried."

To bring this down to earth, after our first year working with Brandon, we went from making $1 million a year and netting $80,000–$100,000, to running a business that did $3.5 million and taking home $500,000. We followed this up the following year, in 2022, by generating $4.5 million and paying ourselves $750,000. Basically, we pulled fifteen years of income forward in two years. So now we're creating a new ten-year goal.

To achieve this growth, we've hired new people to do the things my wife and I used to do. This has meant having to be intentional about our company's culture, which is based on employees believing in their abilities as problem-solvers and teaching others in the business to believe the same. The culture also reflects an abundance mindset that celebrates and expresses gratitude for all of the opportunities we are blessed with as individuals and as a company.

There are two ways we do this. The first is that twice a week, on Mondays and Fridays, we have a 15- to 25-minute "win meeting." Everyone meets at 6 a.m.—we start early in the landscaping business!—and we go around the horn, offering the floor to anyone who wants to share a "win." There are a million different ways to win. People mention a good book they read or movie they watched. Someone might have had a great weekend with their family; someone might talk about a house or yard project they made some headway on. It might be work-related, as, for example, when a crew finished up a job and the client was so happy she brought them a plate of freshly baked cookies.

Then on Fridays, we meet back at the office and share wins from the week. These are more likely to involve work, but might also be personal. We use the win meetings to share our numbers, such as revenues, so everyone can see the progress we're making collectively, from zero dollars on day one of the season to $1 million halfway through, for example. And, of course, everyone can also see where this puts them relative to any bonuses they stand to earn from their hard work. That's inspiring and motivational. The only rule for win meetings is that no one is allowed to get mired in the daily grind or logistics of work. That's what the rest of the day is for!

The second culture-building activity we do is to hold the monthly PPF meetings in which we revisit each team member's personal, professional, and financial goals as they relate to the company's targets and goals. We had one member of the team who had several children and was tired of renting a house. We used our PPF meetings to help him figure out how much he needed to save every month for a down payment on a new house, and I was able to connect him with some friends in the banking community to help him and his wife educate themselves on the finances of home ownership. I've come to see this part of business leadership as critically important, maybe the most important way I've changed since working with Brandon's team.

In addition to changing what we expect from ourselves and our employees, Trista and I have decided to embrace the risk of temporary discomfort for the promise of greater fortune in the future. For years, my wife and I had been sitting on 350 acres of hunting land where we built our home of sixteen years. This year, Trista and I looked at each other and made the decision to sell the home and everything that we have in it, and put ourselves in the state of being uncomfortable. We're going to take the money we make from the land sale and put some of it into our business to help it grow and help our team fulfill their dreams; invest some of it in a new business venture; and we'll take some of the money and put it into passive investments that bring in regular dividends.

If you'd have asked me a couple of years ago whether I ever contemplated taking on a little uncertainty and discomfort like this for the prospect of greater gain later on, I'd have laughed. But we've seen what can happen when you turn wanting more into a belief that the world has everything you could possibly want.

Brandon's programs and processes have given us the framework we needed and the road map to follow to set us up for success through the growth process. We are so grateful to Brandon, his wife, Natalie, Cardone Ventures, and everyone on our Strategic Business Unit Team for helping us navigate the growth of our business and the opportunities we have been given through the growth and abundance mindset that Brandon has shown us.

CHAPTER 14

Thriving in Crisis

Most people go about their daily business trying to do a good job today and, if they have a strategic plan, are working to stick to the plan month after month and year after year. When they think about the future, it is with the hope and expectation that they will have fulfilled certain goals. Most people don't enjoy thinking about the likelihood that some kind of crisis will disrupt their plans and that they'd better be prepared to deal with it. The key is not to wait for the crisis to beset you, but rather to prepare in advance. Because, let's face it, if you have not experienced any sudden trauma, death, personal or professional loss, or profound uncertainty, it's hard to know how you'll feel and behave when things go sideways for reasons out of your control.

All of us were blindsided by the COVID pandemic that struck in the winter and early spring of 2020, and I can attest to having had thousands of clients, friends, colleagues, and others ask me for guidance and advice on navigating this global crisis. My team and I went into overdrive, and, in a three-week period, over a dozen of us rushed to assemble the e-book *The Emergency Business Response*. This chapter represents a "greatest hits" version of that e-book.

Everyone experienced the pandemic differently, so we worked with different clients on different pathways through COVID. You can read about one of those partnerships between my team and a client company called Equipment Experts in the Case Story at the end of this chapter. Their priority involved keeping their operation afloat despite having far too little cash in the bank for those very rainy days of pandemic shutdowns.

At its core, this chapter offers a blueprint for dealing with any crisis from the broadest perspective: the prepared mindset. When I encounter an emergency or crisis, the first thing I do is stop, assess the immediate situation, and then react accordingly. My ability to manage my thinking and my reactions, and the time I have to do so, are the best advantages I have.

Here's the mental checklist I run through:

1. **Am I okay?** In an emergency or crisis, you need to know what your personal situation is. I'm no good to anyone else if I'm not okay and in control of my own mindset and reactions.
2. **Is my family okay?** If you don't have this foundation, nothing else will matter.
3. **Are my friends okay?** Checking in on those you care about will bring comfort and help you decide how you may be able to help.
4. **Are those I'm responsible for okay?** Are your employees, customers, vendors, et al., safe?
5. **How much time do I have to act?** This is the most critical question for your business. If your company is going to fail tomorrow, there's probably not much you can do today. But if you can continue operations for anywhere from a week, a month, or a year (albeit with some drastic changes), take a deep breath. You have the time not only to save but also to strengthen your business—turning crisis into opportunity.
6. **Do I know a trusted resource?** Whenever anything is seriously wrong, our first instinct is to turn to our friends and

family or team or to outside professionals (e.g., attorneys or accountants) and ask what to do. Unless they have been through something similar and proved they could come out better from the situation, this is a bad idea. Instead, you need a trusted resource who has been through circumstances similar to the one you are facing and, most importantly, won.

Even when it seems like the best of times, an emergency or crisis can quickly overtake your business. When it does, how you respond in that moment will define you as a leader. Your reactions and the results they engender will either move you closer to your goals or drive you further away. Business ownership is something many people say they want, but in reality, being a business owner tests you at different times and at all levels to find out if you really have the fortitude to stay in the game at all costs.

People never seem to recognize that business owners only make money when things are going well and there is money left over after expenses. When a company isn't doing well and there is no money to spare, business owners make no money. This is the entry price to business ownership. How a person reacts in an emergency or crisis is what separates a true entrepreneur from the one who is just happy to be his or her own boss. Until a person is staring into the abyss of failure, which might mean being unable to meet payroll, satisfy debt obligations, or deliver on a promise, it is difficult to know just how committed they are.

In my experience, what holds entrepreneurs back from acting decisively when a crisis occurs is that they have not sufficiently prepared themselves—their mindsets—beforehand. Even in the best of times, they try to play it too safe with respect to their people, strategy, and process; thus, it is almost impossible to make the correct decisions at a speed that protects the business today while preserving long-term opportunities. The fact is, a crisis makes thinking harder to do. People become overwhelmed and default to a fight, flight, or freeze response.

For some business owners, emergencies happen every day. They are the result of poor planning, bad advice, inexperience, or circumstances that could have been avoided. That said, when you have a macrodisruption, like the recent global pandemic, everyone is affected across the board. You can only control the controllable; you can't always control what's going on around you. But you can control how you react and respond.

One of the most important controllables involves what I call "context and contrast." To understand what I mean, let's define these terms:

Context: The circumstance s that form the setting for an event, statement, or idea, and the terms in which it can be fully understood and assessed.

Contrast: The state of being strikingly different from something else in juxtaposition or close association.

Keep in mind that making any decision in a state of fear or shock—or making no decisions at all—can create negative momentum that drives you even further into a state of emergency. Worse, reacting the wrong way to short-term problems can drive you into the abyss and move you even further away from your long-term goals.

It is important when confronted with a business emergency to pause for a moment, ask the right questions, and solicit information from trusted resources. Move as fast as you can to assimilate data in order to gain as much context as possible. Until you find data points that you can rely on to confirm or contest your present thinking, pause on making any big decisions. Once you have the appropriate data and knowledge, test your decisions by creating contrasting scenarios to fully think through the steps you will take. Remember, the quality of your questions will always determine the value of the answers.

Stepping back and isolating your decision-making during an emergency—focusing like a laser on what needs to be solved immediately and what decisions you can defer—will also help you slow down. This gives you the time and space necessary to strategically align your current thoughts and actions with your immediate and long-term goals.

Under stress, people tend to make reactive decisions. Reactive change isn't necessarily a bad thing, but it is only valuable when you have used time, energy, and training to react in a calculated and programmatic way that will move you toward the outcome you want. Trained business operators have a systematic, real-time process to formulate the proper response to an emergency. To the inexperienced business owner or leader, it may not be clear what is occurring. It may still look like chaos. But to the trained and experienced eye, all the decision-making activity is executed in a swift, disciplined process.

Sports offer a good parallel to business here. Professional athletes undertake a course of training that enables them and their teams to react in a predictable manner for the best outcome. The members of great teams also have the ability to predict each other's moves, which is essential for winning. But high-performing teams leave little to chance: a basketball team, for example, anticipates having to face a full-court press when the score is close and they lead by a small margin. So they develop plays that meet this new "crisis" in the game by synchronizing every player's actions and roles, allowing them to break the press.

Compare that to most business owners, and you'll see that they have never trained or prepared in this way. When things are going well, most business leaders place little value on training and preparing for emergencies. Obviously, we can't prepare ourselves for every eventuality; sometimes we simply have to spring into action to solve an immediate problem. Knowing when to stop taking action and not overreact is a vital skill, but one usually gained only through training and experience. During times of fear, stress, and anxiety, taking no action or improper actions makes the situation worse, both in the short and long term.

WHY A CRISIS OFTEN CONCEALS
AN OPPORTUNITY

Let's imagine you are in the telemedicine industry. You've spent an enormous amount of time and effort creating a remarkable software product for doctors and patients. But the regulatory issues around the country have been so restrictive, and the rules around medical licensing are so archaic that you can't get people to pay attention to your technology.

Nevertheless, you are ready to go to market. Then a crisis hits that immediately creates fear and anxiety. You overreact. Realizing that you only have enough money to last a few more months, you shut down operations, shelve your plans, let your team go, and retreat from the direction you were heading. I've seen it happen many times.

Then, the president of the country comes on television and says that doctors everywhere are needed because of an emergency. There's going to be a shortage of doctors nationwide. The only fast and safe solution? Telemedicine.

In an instant, the future of telemedicine has shifted for the better. As it turns out, you didn't need to take a long, protracted approach to change all of those rules and regulations, but nonetheless, you missed the opportunity to dominate the market because you prematurely shut down operations.

In moments of contraction, such as those created by pandemics or other crises, the playing field shifts. Many of your competitors will be eliminated because they freeze, flee, or fight incorrectly. Will you join them? The lens you use to view your business opportunities in these times will determine which category you fall into—or choose not to fall into.

With the right mindset, a crisis can be a minor setback or a growth opportunity, one that might even serve as the potential catalyst that propels you to the next level of success, beyond anything you could have imagined before the emergency struck. This is what happened with my client Equipment Experts, noted earlier in the chapter. Not only did we find ways for them not to let COVID bring down the fruits of their efforts, we helped them emerge stronger once the economy began opening up again.

Instead of viewing the situation as a negative, view it as an opportunity. That's what another client, Aaron Christensen, did when he turned his automotive business into a multi-million-dollar business and a dominant player in his space (see the Case Story at the end of chapter 15).

You should see adversity as a way to drive your business forward by recruiting the best available employees, securing a favorable market position, and dominating your current opportunities. If you do so, you will accelerate toward your ideal personal, professional, and financial life. Your whole view on what's happening should change from fear and negativity to positivity and excitement. How you view what's happening right now determines what you do next. And what you do next will eventually define your legacy.

Here's the thing: disruption is a risk all the time, and things will always be happening that have the potential to derail your business— at both macro and micro levels. You must always build your business with the discipline and fortitude needed in good times and bad to plow forward and position yourself with downside protection. Building in these safeguards gives you the best shot to take full advantage of the opportunity, if and when it happens.

Choose to view these circumstances as opportunities, not as liabilities. Look for the little clues that indicate a win. Survive to compete another day and wait patiently to pounce on the bounce back. And when it really matters, ask yourself these questions:

> What mindset do I have during a crisis? Positive or negative?
>
> How prepared am I for an emergency?
>
> How focused am I on the big picture?
>
> How clear am I on my personal, professional, and financial goals?
>
> What is my ideal future picture for myself?
>
> How prepared am I for any disruptions?
>
> How much training have I done to be in a ready state?

The clearer you are in answering these questions *before* disruptions occur, the clearer you will be able to see any hidden opportunities *when* they do. If you keep a cool head, focus on the present, and know what you want your future to look like, you can look at the uncertain situation you're in and recognize whether you are moving toward or away from the things you want.

In a crisis, many business owners immediately disconnect from their ideal personal, professional, and financial goals. A departure from your goals will, in itself, throw you into a state of emotional emergency. You'll begin questioning every decision you ever made and kicking yourself for every opportunity you think you may have missed.

Don't.

Instead, think of yourself as a past, present, and future self, and go from there. Perspective is the best recipe for great decision-making. If all of your thoughts and actions up until now have been foundational to your overall success, a crisis could be the single largest gift ever given to you. Why? Because when things are going well, it's easy to mask problems that could emerge later on to hurt you. If you have an underlying problem or a weak foundation, a crisis will bring that problem into much greater relief.

Fixing the problem could become the biggest opportunity you'll ever see for growth. To do so, however, you have to step back, review the decisions your past self has made, reaffirm what your ideal future success looks like, and use the present moment to keep yourself on course. I call this taking action with intent.

How you view your current situation in a crisis will determine the actions you take. That is the most important lesson of this chapter: make sure your present self actions are consistent with your future self picture. It is one of most important things you need to do before you set yourself into motion.

The best way to align your past, present, and future selves is, again, to build a business with a strong foundation of people, processes, and systems. If you have poor foundational elements in a crisis, you will probably make the wrong choices under pressure. From 2008 to 2012, I watched this happen again and again. Faced with a difficult economic situation, many business owners searching for security went out of business or folded their operations rather than grinding it out. They retreated from owning their own businesses and went back to being employees. They allowed fear to change the trajectory of their lives.

During that same time, I was on the *Inc.* 500 and 5,000 lists of fastest-growing companies (2008–2011). In addition to receiving two awards from *Inc.* for outstanding hiring and employee growth, my company was recognized as the Pacific Northwest's fastest-growing company for five consecutive years. We were eventually awarded three top one hundred workplaces awards, and I received two nominations for entrepreneur of the year.

Those results suggest clear evidence of my mindset at the time: my past negative experiences had emboldened me to take disciplined, intentional actions to secure my market position at all times. For this reason, while others were shutting down, I was aggressively building up. This commitment to the bigger picture eventually propelled me to having my ideal personal, professional, and financial life.

▪ ▪ ▪

Being prepared is a discipline that all business owners should have. Losing all of your revenues for a year is one thing. Having the cash reserves to acquire your biggest competitor is another. Learning how to be prepared in either situation is the best strategy of all.

The best way to secure a healthier future business is to better define your mission, vision, and values. Once you identify what has not been working for you, you can turn those weaknesses into assets. Redefine your mission, vision, and values into actionable, healthy, long-term assets that drive intrinsic worth. If your business has poor employee engagement, an ill-defined culture, a lack of discipline, limited vision into financial indicators, and poorly structured operating processes, you need to change all that going forward. To change your business, you have to first change your perspective, then your words and results will follow, effectively rewriting your own script.

For example, my mission, vision, and values are as follows:

- Mission: To impact the personal, professional, and financial lives of those we serve.
- Vision: To change the way businesses are built by teaching and partnering with business owners to help grow and scale more efficiently, effectively, and profitably.
- Values: inspiration, discipline, accountability, alignment, transparency, and results.

Make what you're moving your future self toward—your purpose—so clear that it's dead simple for everyone involved to understand what your intentions are. Then, once you put that stake in the ground, back it up with the actions that will enable you to achieve those results.

BE CAREFUL WHO YOU TAKE ADVICE FROM

When a crisis strikes, the first thing you should be asking yourself is this: Who am I listening to? Most business leaders struggle with even thinking about crisis response in normal times because they get bad advice from other professionals who don't embody what they want to achieve. No matter who you are listening to, whether it's peers, friends, employees, lawyers, family members, advisors, accountants, or consultants, you should be asking yourself the following questions:

Are these people living, breathing examples of what I'm trying to do?

Have they done it before?

Have they written books or papers on it? Have they experienced it themselves?

Have they built what I want to build?

Do they have the credibility that comes with successful execution?

As my dear friend Adam La Reau would say, "Who you're mentored by, study under, associate with, train with, trust, and ultimately go to battle with will determine the quality of your outcomes."

Adam is a retired US Navy SEAL with two Bronze Stars, nine Service and two Combat Action Ribbons, and three Presidential Unit Citations and one Navy Unit Citation. Someone like Adam is the kind of expert you want to learn from when the crap hits the fan, especially when it comes to creating a process for dealing with emergencies.

When I asked Adam to name the one thing leaders should remember during a crisis, he replied, "As leaders, people are looking to you to see how to respond to and react in times of uncertainty. Oftentimes, they see you as the person who either keeps calm or freaks out under pressure. When your employees, family, peers, vendors, bankers, or customers see how you react, they will react the same way.

As we explored this further, Adam emphasized that you can't prepare for every possible eventuality. Every shot you take, mountain you climb, plane you jump out of, and ocean you dive into differs from every other one. The environment is constantly changing. The enemy is always trying to outsmart you, and you need to constantly adapt not just to survive but to thrive, win, and make it home safe, mission after mission, deployment after deployment.

Often you don't know exactly what you're up against or what you can't physically accomplish during a given time. When you're overwhelmed, you have the potential to view everything as a threat. Doing this will strain your decision-making, simply because you can't maintain a heightened sense of awareness for extremely long periods of time.

As a leader, your job is to see further, faster. That said, you don't need to solve every problem. The most important assets that give you strength during challenging times are the warriors standing next to you. It's about the team. As a unit, you are collectively stronger.

Adam's advice is to focus on getting 1 percent better every day. He challenges each of us to remember that business success is not a sprint. It is a marathon. In order to endure through challenging times, you have to focus on what you can control. Maintain a positive mental attitude and warrior spirit. Dig in, take ground, and when the crisis passes, you and your organization will come out stronger on the other side.

For additional resources, get immediate access to exclusive behind the scenes videos that uncover even more items I couldn't share in this book. To access these exclusive resources, visit NineFigureTools.com

Crisis Management Cash Flow to the Rescue

Stacy Conner, Equipment Experts Inc., Owner

When someone dropped a block of concrete on my husband, Greg's, foot and knocked him out of work, I had just delivered our third child via C-section. Our house was basically an infirmary. While we were trying to figure out our next move as a family, Greg, who is a heavy equipment field mechanic, took care of the kids and, during his spare time, bought an old truck chassis for a few thousand dollars and started building it out as an equipment repair truck in our driveway. By the time he finished, he had installed toolboxes and a compressor, welder, crane, and everything you'd need to service big equipment at a construction jobsite. He even installed a microwave oven to heat up meals.

In 2005, Greg started Equipment Experts with just the one truck and a determination to succeed. He had tried to go out on his own in his early twenties, but it hadn't worked out. This time around, we weren't going to let that happen. Greg had been a mechanic since he was sixteen years old and was very independent-minded and confident of his ability to bull his way through any mechanical problem in the universe, so for several years, working seventeen-hour days, six or seven days a week, is what he did.

The problem was that he had never had to hire or manage other people. All he knew about was how to work hard. I worked in marketing at a corporation, but quit to work with Greg. I had a bachelor's degree in business and understood marketing and sales better than he did, but I didn't have any real management experience either. We had a unique business, which was to outfit trucks like Greg had done in our driveway and send them to worksites to fix trucks, forklifts, and heavy equipment. Our niche was that our trucks functioned as mobile repair shops with everything needed to do any job. Customers didn't have to bring their equipment into a shop and leave it there.

Over a three- or four-year period, we built fifteen more trucks and hired people to work them, as well as some office staff. We grew, too, going from $400,000 in revenues to $4,000,000. This may sound good, but we were always cash-poor from having to lay out $100,000 at a time to buy and equip a truck. The answer always seemed to be to build more trucks. The problem was that they weren't profitable. We struggled with cash flow and never had more than $80,000 to $100,000 in reserve.

I worked for free for three years. I paid for health insurance for everybody else, but our family had catastrophic-only health insurance for a few years. We were determined to make it no matter what, but just weren't able to get out from being slaves to our business. We hired some consultants, but they focused on functional stuff. They coached us to build the company, but they weren't experts on the business side of the business or on managing a team.

After many years of this, in 2015, a friend of a friend introduced me to Grant Cardone's book *The 10X Rule: The Only Difference between Success and Failure.* Greg and I went to Grant's 10X Growth

Conference for the first time in 2020. Everything about the book spoke to what we had been feeling: that we wanted to break through to a new level of understanding how we could be successful. We were sitting there with thirteen thousand people, and Brandon Dawson came on stage and did a presentation. He said the growth of a business is an algorithmic, step-by-step process that you can follow—and if you do, your business will grow and be profitable.

That's what had been missing! Was it possible we wouldn't have to keep running into the same wall over and over again?

Greg and I talked to Brandon, and he was very pointed when we told him about the things we'd tried to do and hadn't been successful at with the business. Brandon suggested working with him.

"Why wouldn't you?" he asked us.

So we did.

No sooner had the excitement of 10X Growth Convention 2020 and meeting Brandon ended than COVID struck, a crisis we were absolutely ill-equipped to handle. And no sooner had we signed on with Brandon than he was walking us through a major emergency. When the pandemic started closing things down, I completely freaked out. We had $100,000 in the bank. That wasn't enough to get a company of twenty-five people through a crisis.

I was scared, and coming from a place of having lived with chronic anxiety and stress, I had a tendency to catastrophize. So instead of being calm and getting through a thing, I was in a panic. When one of the co-owners is in a panic, it sets the tone for the rest of the company.

"Okay, first thing we do," said Brandon, "is to increase our line of credit, and, since banks have a tendency to close those lines of credit during a crisis, to pull the cash immediately." We did this and our bank account quadrupled in size. In the meantime, I found out we could employ our team on an as-needed basis during the pandemic so they could also collect unemployment. We got Payment Protection Plan money to help us through. I was able to save all of their benefits, all their vacation time, keep their health insurance in place, and get the whole company through the crisis.

We followed a lot of Brandon's emergency business response protocol, including the lifeboat drill, which resulted in keeping 90 percent of our team. The lifeboat drill involves evaluating your team in terms of operational effectiveness, belief, and leadership in the company. Belief refers to the person's demonstration of your values and shared goals. You run the exercise again without the belief component, and when we did that the same four people panned out significantly below the others. We cut them and the company became better for it, even though it was painful to do because I strive to be loyal to people. But sometimes that's not in the best interest of the company. And we cut people who had not been contributing to the level that they should have been—people we should have cut earlier.

We also used our relationship with Brandon to train our staff to become even more valuable in terms of operational effectiveness, belief, and leadership. We work in a tough industry that is experiencing a shortage of highly skilled and experienced mechanics. The old days of young people learning the trade in garages with their dads and uncles and friends are coming to end. More and more young people are going into video games and electronics, which poses a serious labor issue. We've been exploring some innovative ways of delivering new kinds of training, but we're also working with Brandon's team to upgrade our team's skill sets across the board.

Maybe the biggest lesson I learned from COVID was that the best way to avert a crisis is to understand the financial rules of running a profitable and growing business. The work we did with Brandon has positively impacted every area of our business and put us in a much better position than we were in just two years ago. Our revenues are up 46 percent, but even more important is that our cash flow is solid enough to get us through whatever fresh crisis comes our way.

The most significant part of working with Brandon and Cardone Ventures has been getting that 60,000-foot perspective we lacked for so many years. If you're in a place where you can't see what the end looks like, whether or not a crisis precipitated it, you have a tendency to see nothing but gloom and doom as the outcome. Not only that, you tend to hear mostly about the shipwrecks. But if you're lucky, you meet the salty sailor who was just out for six months and went through five hurricanes and walked into a bar, sat down, and ordered a beer.

That sailor is Brandon.

CHAPTER 15

Create for Tomorrow— Live for Today

Most of us have an innate desire to reach our potential. The problem is that this desire to grow and develop makes us discontent with the way things are in the here and now. Our feelings about life and happiness revolve around three main beliefs that prevent our feeling satisfied with the present. First, we believe that the things we don't have are better than those we do have. It's the old "grass is greener on the other side of the fence" belief. The second belief is that regardless of what we have, having more of it is always better. And the third belief holds that when we get what we want, we will be happy at last.

Are these beliefs true? Maybe a better way to phrase the question would be, "Does thinking this way work as a means of reaching a desired state of happiness and fulfillment?" As you can probably surmise, I think the answer is probably not, for a specific reason that I call the fallacy of the success ethic. If we refer to the third belief, we see the essence of the fallacy at work: when you get what you want, you will be happy. If you work hard and solve all of the problems in your life, happiness will be yours. As a result of the success ethic, which is the model that most people in our society apply to their lives (whether consciously or unconsciously), we believe that if we *have* the things that happy people have, we will *do* what happy people do. Then, of course, it follows that we will also *be* happy.

Let's call this the Having-Doing-Being flow of fulfillment.

You and I have more of everything than any generation before on this planet. We have more time to do what we want, more money to spend on what we want, and more labor-saving advanced technology than any civilization in history. Yet, as a culture, we are far from happy or satisfied. One of the major problems lies in the flow of the success ethic from Having into Doing into Being. The universe works differently, flowing instead from Being into Doing into Having.

How does this work? We believe that having what we think we want will help us to be able to do the things we want to do, which will help us to *be* who we want to be—a happy person. But life unfolds in an opposite cause-and-effect relationship: people who are busy *being* happy are the ones who are doing what they love to do and, in turn, receiving what they want to have.

This principle applies as much to business as it does to life. In fact, most small to midsize business owners started their companies using the Being-Doing-Having model. They thought of an idea that included seeing themselves as business owners. They started working and investing their money and time into the business. Their early focus on the task of achieving and staying in business was so profound that they didn't think much about all the things they could accumulate during the building process. They were busy Doing. Then, when they had the income to obtain the things they had dreamed of having, they became distracted by wanting more. Their mindset shifted to Having-Doing-Being.

Consider the analogy of a struggling actor working hard for years getting small parts and perfecting the craft of acting. One day, the big break comes and the actor is recognized as a star. The danger here is that the actor will no longer focus on being an actor and doing what actors do—prepare, study, learn from other actors—and become obsessed with becoming an A-list star. It isn't enough to be *one* of the top-billed actors; this actor must be *the* top-billed actor. Once top billing is achieved, the actor is still dissatisfied because of the need for an Oscar. Once the Oscar is won, the actor becomes obsessed with winning another one. In the meantime, this actor no longer enjoys being an actor in the same way as before, even though he's the envy of hundreds of thousands of other actors.

The same syndrome often besets entrepreneurs. Most of them say, "The first few years when I was just starting my business were the most fun. Everything was new and exciting." Even though they didn't have any money and didn't know if they would stay afloat, they were excited by being in charge of their own destiny and throwing themselves into the role of business owner. Their expectations were tempered, and everything they did felt like an accomplishment. Just being in business day-to-day spelled success for them. Once the business grew, however, they grew disappointed and felt handcuffed to it. They also began to grow defensive, focusing on the things that they didn't want to lose rather than on what they needed to do to continue growing. They lost the joy of experimentation and discovery that comes from taking risks and investing in new opportunities. The fun and excitement were exchanged for fear, disappointment, and frustration. How did this happen?

THE PROVERBIAL CARROT

If you say, "I'll be happy when . . . ," you will never be happy. It becomes the carrot at the end of the stick that you can never quite reach. Suppose the time comes when you get that thing you thought would make you happy. It makes no difference in the way you feel. Then you have to find something else to make you happy. The better bet is to focus on feeling happy from the inside out rather than to derive your joy from external objects and possessions. If you are happy from the inside out, you will begin doing what happy people do and you will have what happy people have. For me, it's been the continuous pursuit of adding value to people's lives. That makes me happy every day, not the actual monetary results that come from it.

One of the Buddha's greatest contributions was his teaching that desire creates suffering. When you want something and you don't appreciate what you already have, you suffer. Now, this doesn't mean that you shouldn't create more abundance—more money, more friends, more adventures, more joy—in your life. But so many of us are unhappy no matter how much we gain. We always seem to want what we don't have, and when we finally get what we want, it's like the Peggy Lee song, "Is That All There Is?"

Of course, living in the present doesn't mean that you just accept what you have and cease to create and cease to explore. It simply means that you already have what you want at the Being level. In other words, you are already a success *right now*. That perfection is who you are at the Being level, and your happiness stems from that spiritual perfection. Getting what you want cannot change your life at the Being level, so don't let what you have determine *who you are*.

You may ask, "If it's all about Being, why do anything at all?" Remember that the model is Being-Doing-Having. If you are Being happy and satisfied from the inside out, you will start Doing what happy and satisfied people do. Then, and only then, will you Have what happy and satisfied people have. There is no specific dollar amount attached to this model because each of our needs and goals are different; yours are your own. When you proceed from a spiritually contented place, what you do from there will be motivated by confidence in who you are rather than by fear of who you are not or who you want to be. In that state of mind—in that mindset— you will be able to desire things without feeling that you don't have enough right now.

Remember my story about building a business to prove to my family that I could do it? That desire had nothing to do with who I really was. All of us seek some measure of approval or appreciation from others, but I was seeking validation, which meant that I was effectively living someone else's life rather than my own. Once I stepped back and understood what I had been doing, I could appreciate that I no longer wanted to be that person. Everything I did after that felt right and natural. When your happiness isn't predicated on what you do, you are much freer to do what you want. You can explore and discover from a place of excitement. That's when you can truly find and express your passion.

THE MOMENT OF NOW IS WHERE THE POWER LIES

The more focused we remain on Having something, the more our lives become focused on solving problems that stand in the way. This can be an exhausting way to live every day, which explains why, following the first flush of love with entrepreneurship, entrepreneurs often begin to have a harder time getting themselves out of bed in the morning to face yet another day of problem-solving for themselves, plus their employees, family members, friends, and the rest of the world. Solving problems is rewarding if that's what you love to do, but too many of the problems we face aren't the ones we relish tackling. They're trite and onerous and, even worse, blind us to the things we already have.

The problem arises when we believe that having what we think we want will help us do the things we want to do, which will in turn help us to be who we want to be. Life unfolds in the opposite cause-and-effect relationship: people who are busy being happy are the ones who are doing what they love to do and, in turn, receiving what they want to have. The same principle applies to business life. Most owners of small to midsize businesses start their companies because they see themselves as business owners. They focus so intently on building their business that they don't think about accumulating things—of Having.

Once they make more money, they begin to want to have more and more things until they reach the point when they fall out of love with "being" a business owner and begin living for the far-off day when they will "have" all that they desire and will therefore be a happy and fulfilled person. They've got it wrong, however, because life is a journey, not a destination, and they will not get back those years they lost living only for the future.

The answer lies in creating for tomorrow but living in, and for, today. This means having that ironclad ten-year picture of where you're ultimately going to be ten years out so that you can simultaneously drive toward that goal *and* enjoy the fact that you are experiencing movement toward your dream each and every day. For example, every time Natalie and I get on our jet, we have to shake ourselves a little. We're living a life we couldn't have dreamed of before dedicating ourselves to our ten-year vision (which, by the way, is not even halfway through being realized).

The vast majority of us are not islands; we are family members and friends and teammates. We need to spend time with all the people who make our lives what they are. If your personal time is spent almost entirely trying to unwind from the stress of work, you'll have little of value left to offer those other folks. You already know my personal story of learning this lesson the hard way, as a child, husband, and parent. No matter how frustrating it can be to shut off the world and pay 100 percent attention to your family—or whatever is most important to you on a personal level—trust me, it's worth it. And know this: your family and friends are far more hurt by your distraction than you can possibly know.

So make a choice: enjoy what you have today while working for tomorrow, or stress out over what you don't have and live only for tomorrow. Personally, I feel that living only for tomorrow doesn't offer much of a future. Avoid the trap that results in so many failing businesses, unhappy marriages, and dysfunctional families. Don't lose sight of what matters.

IMPLEMENTING A PLAN OF ACTION

Let's stop here for a moment and address the elephant in the room: How do you solve problems without focusing on them? How do you set goals and live in the moment at the same time? As you begin to notice where you place your focus on a daily basis and how you fail to enjoy the present moment, you will begin to see that you absolutely *can* enjoy what you have while still setting goals for the future. It's possible to live for today while still planning for tomorrow, if what you are planning involves creating something that fulfills your sense of purpose in life. That something might be the solution of a problem, but it is a problem that fascinates you just as much as the prospect of solving it does.

Focusing on what you want to create expresses enthusiasm for the future, not discontent with the present. It requires that you set goals and determine where you want to go. If you aren't achieving what you're capable of achieving, you may not be setting the kind of goals that clearly define a path forward. When you set a goal, you make a choice to go in one direction rather than another one and to focus on doing one thing rather than another.

"Ah," you might say, shaking your head. "But I don't want to be pinned down. There are so many projects in my head. I want to be spontaneous. I want to be free to change my mind. You said to 'stay in the moment,' so why plan anything?"

Well, sometimes we mistakenly think that freedom means avoiding commitment. We fear that if we commit to something, it will own and control us. Some people refer to this as "optionality," which is keeping your options open in anticipation of greater things around the corner. If the business owner maintains this optionality mindset too long, however, his or her employees will develop the mindset as well. I see business owner after business owner frustrated when their employees don't set or reach goals. What the owners fail to realize is that they have established this culture themselves. It's patterned after them.

The first mistake we make in this situation is believing that a commitment to a goal means we can't change our minds. Not true. Part of being a business leader is not only being able to commit to one course of action but also being able to self-correct when the course doesn't lead where it's supposed to lead. In other words, great leaders are great learners and adapters as well as confident decision-makers. If something isn't working, you can alter the goal, but if you set no goal at all, you may as well travel in circles. Real freedom actually lies in our ability to make choices and commitments.

TO MAKE IT COUNT, WRITE IT DOWN

Not only must you set goals, you've also got to write them down. The kinetic action of writing will further impress your ideas into your subconscious. Your written plan will give you the courage to follow through and will help you eliminate obstacles, distractions, and interruptions. It will also serve as a yardstick for your progress. You will be more aware of how far you have come and how far you have to go. Psychological studies have shown that measuring your progress not only enables you to stay on course to reach your goals, it actually motivates you to a higher degree.

Writing crystallizes thought, and thought motivates action. It reinforces your commitment to attain what you want, reminds you of your objectives, and serves as a marker along your journey. And when obstacles get in your way, your written plan will help you to reevaluate and get back on track.

Written documentation of your goals is a must for your business and for every person on your staff. Many business owners I have met don't make this a focal point. Then they wonder why their staff doesn't experience greater success. Goal-setting must be built into your company's culture, operations, and overall strategy. And the best way to set goals is to leave nothing to chance interpretation.

To make it count, set the target and write it down.

THE HIGH PRICE OF INDECISION

We have all been programmed since childhood not to make mistakes, and making decisions exposes the decision-maker to the possibility of error. I see this dynamic at work among middle managers who don't want to make a bad choice they feel will incur the business owner's displeasure. They tend to allow their staff to try to figure things out themselves and, when things work, take the credit for it. I'm not advocating micromanagement, but I do believe that failing to make decisions for fear of being wrong hurts companies. When this happens, your business becomes paralyzed and incapable of moving in any direction.

People also avoid making decisions for fear of displeasing others. Choosing one thing over other things means you can't be everything to everybody. When you make a choice, you run the risk of rejecting the values of people who see a different side of you than they did when you were indecisive and thus, at least superficially, more agreeable to them. The truth is that we have no choice but to make choices—and even not making a choice is making a choice.

IDENTIFYING THE BENEFITS

So far, I may have appeared to argue that the most important part of goal-setting is, well, setting a goal. But it's not. The most important step in goal-setting is identifying benefits to you that will come from achieving your goal. This is true of business, and it's true of relationships. If you're unsure of the benefits of an action, how can you get your employees behind it?

Throughout the years, when my companies have gone on-site to interview a business owner's staff, we found that, as a rule, no one in the organization was making sure that their personal benefits were incorporated into the daily routine of the business. I don't mean a standard benefit package, such as health care, insurance, 401(k), etc. I'm referring to the personal benefit to the individual of having a project succeed: praise, a bonus, a promotion, or a raise. The owners are frustrated because their employees are not achieving the goals of the company; the employees are frustrated because they're not getting anything they want. No one is on the same page about the plan or shared vision because there is no common goal.

Goal-setting helps you to specifically identify the benefits you will receive from the efforts you expend. It also helps you to outline the benefits to each employee. Take note that you want to make sure you include personal, professional, and financial goals covering the short term, medium term, and long term in order to apply a balanced approach to the employee's life. What will be the payoff for each specific staff member if they reach a particular goal? One of the easiest and quickest benefits of goal-setting is the positive feedback you give to your employees.

Don't try to keep each and every mile marker in your head; keep a (written) list of the goals you accomplish and note the obstacles that had to be overcome in the process. For a copy of the goal tracker we use at Cardone Ventures, use the QR code in the photo. As you complete your goals, file your written notes in your notebook, review them periodically, and (most importantly) when you win, celebrate!

Keep adding to your list of accomplished goals. Every time you look at this list, you will gain further confidence in your ability to obtain what you want through goal-setting. And don't hog all the confidence and good feelings for yourself. Share your list with your team and let them know how much you appreciate them.

If this all seems like a lot of extra effort on your part, rest assured that it represents a far, far more efficient use of your time than going through life without a road map. Don't be fooled by the apparent simplicity of this process. Goal-setting is your blueprint for success. It's also a habit that will reward you for the rest of your life. Incorporate this as standard protocol in your organization.

ABOVE ALL . . . GET STARTED!

Committing to a goal only makes sense, of course, as long as the goal makes sense. There's no point in sticking with a goal that no longer aligns with what you are truly passionate about and motivated by. You can change your mind anytime you want. But for the moment, the important thing is to *get started*. You will fail to reach 100 percent of the goals you never set for yourself. Don't wallow in the mire of optionality and hypotheticals until you lose all the momentum you gained by deciding to create something new, like a business. There is no substitute for momentum.

In time, too many entrepreneurs become overwhelmed by the distance of their goal and give up. Remember that every large goal is the sum total of the smaller goals that you achieve on the way. Concentrate on each milestone before moving on, mentally and emotionally, to the next one. Use your overall goal as a point of reference as you work on accomplishing each smaller goal. Here is a formula for successful goal-setting I've used to start projects:

1. Start: What do I want? Be clear and specific.
2. Assess: Am I doing the things necessary to move in the direction of what I want?
3. Adapt: What changes do I need to make to do it bigger, better, and faster?
4. Measure: How am I tracking accountability and execution?
5. Increase intensity: (Re)focus on what matters most.

6. Assess again.
7. Adapt some more.
8. Measure again.
9. Duplicate: When my efforts produce positive results, train others to replicate them.
10. Create anew: Once my team has mastered my process, step back and ask, "What next?"

I've worked with thousands of individuals and businesses, and do you know what? This method of goal-setting has proven itself every time.

For additional resources, get immediate access to exclusive behind the scenes videos that uncover even more items I couldn't share in this book. To access these exclusive resources, visit NineFigureTools.com

Riding Out the Ups and Downs at Christensen Automotive Repair Services

Aaron Christensen, Owner

I was born into a family that ran a mom-and-pop business called Christensen Automotive Repair Services in South Lake Tahoe, Nevada. My parents, Rich and Wendy Christensen, started the business in 1998, and I worked there in high school, changing oil and working myself up to bigger jobs. My parents tried to open new garages but usually wound up selling them off because it was too hard to manage multiple stores. After spending eight years on active duty in the Air Force following high school, I moved home and joined the family business.

When I joined the company full-time, my dad told me he was having a hard time finding and keeping good employees, so I kept this in mind in my job there, which was running the service desk—the place where people came up to explain what they needed so I could assign a work order for them. That proved an excellent vantage point to observe how everything ran. Having me there gave my parents confidence to open a second store in Gardnerville in 2001, a third store in Carson City in 2008, and a fourth store in Reno in 2012, which was also the year my brother Bryan returned from military service to join us in the business.

Fast-forward to 2015, when Bryan and I bought out our parents and gave them the retirement they richly deserved. With our military backgrounds, Bryan and I were thinking in terms of how to develop more leadership throughout our business to overcome the problems we'd had keeping our best people. Small garages don't tend to develop an aptitude for growth and expansion. The best technicians typically leave and open their own small garages. Unless you happen to have other stars in the waiting, you have to go out and find someone new, which takes time and costs a lot.

We wanted to create a way for our best people to grow. By 2018, any kind of progress on this front came to a halt when I was called up to serve in the National Guard and was deployed to the Middle East. During this time, the business began to struggle, and it was hard to put our finger on exactly why, especially with me halfway across the globe.

When I returned in 2019, we learned about Cardone Ventures and attended one of its boot camps in Aventura, Florida. Our goal was to find someone who could help us think through the people management side of Christensen. As soon as Grant Cardone and Brandon Dawson got up on stage and began talking about business growth and learning to lead so that your company worked *for* you rather than the other way around, I knew I could trust these guys. You take a couple of military guys like my brother and me, and you have two people who are oriented toward serving. And that's what we were doing: constantly solving everyone's problems and making life a bit too easy for our employees. So I joined the Zoom call Brandon hosted and, by late 2019, business began to turn around.

Not only did I learn from the insights Brandon offered about measuring everything we did, I learned quite a bit from the other business owners who were experiencing some of the same problems we were.

Within a short time, I felt a fog lifting from my mind as the operations of our garages suddenly grew clearer to me. We had always functioned pretty much without writing anything down. We kept everything in our heads, which wasn't very effective. We began tracking the amount of work being referred to different mechanics to see how efficiently we were making use of our billable hours.

And we discovered some extreme imbalances in productivity. Sometimes the imbalances stemmed from service people referring more work to some mechanics than to others; in other cases, it was due to one mechanic taking a lot longer to complete a job than his colleagues. Understanding where inefficiencies came from made it much easier to raise the level of the whole garage. We evaluated each of our five garages in a systematic way. We let go of some of our weakest performers and spread their hours among the top performers. By January of 2020, we had money in the bank and were looking to really thrive. We were working with Brandon and began thinking about making a move to grow again and add new locations.

And then COVID kicked us in the teeth.

They say luck is when preparation meets opportunity. Well, with enough money to take care of our employees, we tightened up our business systems and processes and waited out the worst of the pandemic. When the economy and society opened up again, we were in a good position to expand. We had been doing a couple of million a year before Brandon began working with us. Once he started working with us, in the course of eighteen months, we began doing almost $8 million in two locations. And then, because we had our business cranking, we generated enough cash to buy out a competitor with twelve locations, again with help from Brandon.

We wound up parting ways with a number of employees, which was very expensive since we figured out it cost around $250,000 in lost revenue and outreach to replace each one. We poured ourselves into a recruitment effort that was documented and methodical. We were ruthless in our standards for who we hired, and we also implemented an employee maturity model, recommended by Cardone Ventures, that provided clear pathways for promotion and success for everyone at Christensen Automotive. We had been sabotaging ourselves by allowing employees to assume they understood what was expected of them. Some more or less did; most did not. And we had only ourselves to blame.

Not anymore.

This was a painful time, not least because I spent a lot of weeks out of each month away from home. In addition, in the midst of trying to integrate the competitor into our business, one of my partners left the company, which compounded the amount of energy, work, and emotion being expended. Fortunately, Brandon kept our heads in the game and helped keep us focused on taking action toward the stated objectives without getting caught up in the dynamics or politics or emotion of everything. We were able to turn that business around and then sell it on the other side of COVID for a substantial amount of money.

In fact, our sale was so successful that I received enough to provide something that Brandon always told us was the most important lesson about getting money: "It's about earning the ultimate freedom to do what you want, when you want, and with whom you want," he always said.

That's what I wanted. And I'm there now. I'm thirty-nine years old, and I've got a lot of gas left in the tank. I'll definitely start another business. It probably won't be in the automotive industry, but now I feel confident enough in myself as a businessman to be successful at something I didn't literally grow up doing. We'll go find another business where we can do the same thing.

I may have chosen the military over going to college, but the amount of stuff we've learned in the last three years working with Brandon has been like earning a doctorate in the practical application of growing a small business.

The Nine-Figure Mindset

By this point in the book, you've learned about my journey and the lessons I've gleaned along the way as an entrepreneur, founder, and business owner. You've read some chapters devoted to developing the habits and perspectives you need to establish your own nine-figure mindset. I hope you've learned not only a lot of the things you should do to reach your goals, but also a lot of the things you shouldn't do to avoid experiencing some of the setbacks I experienced. On top of all this, you have heard from other business owners who have experienced the same doubts and challenges as you may have had or continue to have *right now*. I think you'll agree that they are some pretty amazing people.

But I'm here to tell you that none of them are more amazing than you will be when you commit yourself to the belief that you are going to let absolutely nothing stop you from achieving your dreams and goals, and even more so when you teach those around you to do the same. Outflow amplifies inflow!

■ ■ ■

Remember, the whole point of this book is to give you the inspiration, courage, and road map to develop your own nine-figure mindset. The Law of Attraction takes effect when you apply the Law of Intention, then the Law of Action—then you attract. The exact "how" of it isn't as important right now as making the commitment to yourself, visualizing it, and then taking action toward your stated objective. Then, voilà! You attract it. The whole process of building a nine-figure mindset begins with not becoming overwhelmed when you haven't even hit six figures yet!

Here's how to get yourself on the right pathway and keep yourself on course:

1. **Build a relationship with someone who is interested in mentoring you into success.** Find an example of somebody who has done something you want to do, study them, and then emulate to the best of your abilities what they did to become successful. If you are a dentist and you want to build a multi-million-dollar practice that you can sell, you should not be talking to anyone who hasn't done exactly that—not a nickel more or less than your goal, no matter how big it is—and is willing and able to teach you how to do it.

2. **Decide how big a problem you can solve right now.** The pathway to nine figures doesn't begin by saying to yourself, "I want to be worth $100 million." Your pathway to nine figures must be undertaken incrementally—one zero at a time. In order to develop a nine-figure mindset, you must first develop a six-figure mindset, then a seven-figure mindset, and so on. If you can't make $100,000, you can't make $1 million, and if you can't make $1 million, you certainly can't make $10 million. Your first $100,000 is totally controlled by how you think and what you do as a producer. Your first $1 million of income is controlled by how you think, what you do, and how many people you can inspire to come do it with you based on knowing *how* you made that $100,000. Your eight-figure achievement comes through multiplying and amplifying through the teams of people you

build to solve the problems you've identified as worth solving through your products or services.

To be clear, when you establish your intention statements, having $100 million net worth is different than having $100 million of cash sitting in your account. You need to be crystal clear in your intention. For example, saying, "It is my intention to have $100 million dollar net worth" is different than saying, "My intention is to have $100 million in cash in the bank."

Once people establish their intentions and dedicate themselves to action, the hardest thing for human beings in all aspects of their lives is to have the discipline and resilience to never give up pursuing and hitting their target.

Remember, in order for you to be able to teach others to do something, you have to have been able to master it yourself. In effect, what most people refer to as "scale" basically means leading and collaborating with larger and larger groups of people.

Once you've mastered this skill of multiplying and amplifying and your business is effectively working for you (rather than the other way around), you are ready to 10X what you have already been doing. And that is how you get to the nine-figure mindset.

3. **Ask the right people.** In addition to looking to your mentor or model for what you want to accomplish and deciding at what mile marker (or dollar marker) in your journey you can realistically begin, broaden your network of people who are willing to answer your questions. However, in doing so, only ask questions of people who have demonstrated that they have actually done what you are trying to do. If you want to make $10 million, only talk to people who have made that amount of money. It's far less important that they actually be in your market than that they have built a business to the value to which you want to build.

There is way too much free advice being touted by people who want to make a name for themselves recommending things they have never actually succeeded in doing. Even if they mean well, do not look to them for guidance. If you are at $3 million and want to make $100 million, do not seek guidance, advice, mentorship, or wisdom from anyone who has not made $100 million. Only seek guidance, polling, opinion, perspective, strategy, or structure from people who have actually done it and are willing to share with you how they did it. With that said, it is okay to ask in stages. If you are at $3 million and you get advice from someone who makes $10 million, that's fine, but realize that once you get close to hitting those numbers, you will need to move to a new mentor. This is crucial, and John Maxwell describes this in "Law of the Lid," the first chapter of *The 21 Irrefutable Laws of Leadership*.

4. **Master the "seven promotes."** In order to start and build your business, you have to master what I call the seven promotes. *First,* promote what you do. *Second,* promote why you do it—your passion. *Third,* promote who you do it *for*. *Fourth,* promote the impact that somebody working with you should expect to receive (i.e., a value proposition). *Fifth,* promote the benefits to those who choose to join your team and do it with you. *Sixth,* promote your people to take over your roles and responsibilities so you can work on the business versus in it. *Seventh,* promote and teach everyone on your team to do the first six promotes!

The highest level of promotion is when you get your teams and clients all promoting these promotes into the marketplace. The promotion of your people and your clients will take your business to explosive growth. All of your short and long term thinking should be around how to get your people and customers to do the promotion for you because your impact on their lives is significant.

The important point to remember here is that the habit of promoting never ends; it simply becomes amplified and multiplied through the process we discussed earlier in the book: modeling, mimicking, mastering, and multiplying.

5. **Diversify your product base.** As you are building your teams and you move from six figures to seven, eight, and nine figures, start looking at products and services you can add to your customer base so that the relationships you've already built can do more business with you than just one or two things.

6. **Build your business to value.** While you are building your business, duplicating systems and processes by modeling, mimicking, mastering, and multiplying through your teams while following the seven promotes, take the time to go out into the marketplace and arrive at a sense of the value of your business at the present time. Use industry networks, research with search engines like Google, or identify businesses like yours that have sold recently to find out how much your business is worth. This is important because you are not only building income with every passing year, you are also building equity value in your business.

Remember, there are different ways to get to nine figures: you can get there through income, you can there through revenue, and you can get there through value. Each of these measures something different. For example, if you have a $100 million company, it may only be worth $40 million or $50 million if you build it wrong. Having a $100 million company is entirely different than having a $100 million net worth. And having a $100 million net worth is entirely different than having $100 million in cash sitting in the bank.

7. **Exit at high value.** If you are studying your market every year and paying attention to the value of your business (which you can do by finding out who is selling and talking to different brokers in the marketplace), you will become aware of the cycles in which all businesses, including yours, operate. Your business may be worth more one year than the previous year, then go back to being worth less in the next year. The closer attention you pay to the fluidity of the valuations in

your market year over year, the higher chance you will have of exiting at the highest value. The best reference for this step is in *Exit Rich: The 6 P Method to Sell Your Business for Huge Profit,* by Michelle Seiler Tucker and my mentor Sharon Lechter.

▪ ▪ ▪

The whole purpose of building a business is for it to perform in a way that allows the courageous founder to live their dream life by accomplishing their stated goals. The business is also responsible to be a utility for your team members to achieve their personal, professional, and financial goals through the business. The owner and leaders must force the business to conform to doing its job. The business consists of you and your team, and it exists to provide remarkable value for your products and service—such remarkable value, in fact, that you and your team will contribute 100 percent of your attention and activities to the success of the business. If this sounds like a heady brew, rest assured it is a very heady brew indeed. But that is the secret to building a business. That's the purpose of business: to provide a remarkable life to those who invest in its success!

Remember this: building a great business begins and ends with you and your determination to be more, do more, and have more. But accomplishing this worthiest of pursuits is not something that you undertake alone. You can't and shouldn't ever try to do it by yourself. The highest value and richest rewards—and the fastest way to become successful—come through collaboration. Collaboration *is* the new global currency. Invest in it today, tomorrow, and forever, and do it wisely, and your blessings will always outnumber your regrets.

If you are truly committed to 10Xing your life and want to be an example to others around you, you must be entirely *unreasonable* with your current conditions and never settle or make excuses for where you are now at the expense of moving boldly to where you're dedicated to going.

MESSAGE FROM BRANDON DAWSON

Thanks for taking the time to read *Nine Figure Mindset*—I hope you enjoyed it. This is the first of a series of books that I'll be publishing as simple guidebooks full of tips, strategies, and advice on the fastest path for you to generate a nine-figure net worth and a massive impact in your marketplace with your business.

Scaling can be easier if you know the science behind it, especially knowing what to do and what NOT to do. Having bad advice or even none at all can set you back years, if not decades. Mindset is where it starts, but it's crucial you find the right mentors to show you the path of least resistance, and I'm excited to be a mentor for you.

I know when I was forced out of one of my companies just because I had made one little mistake, I would have done anything to know what I know now because it cost me millions. I'm not going to let that happen to you, so to carry your momentum from this book, I would like to invite you to access a private forty-minute training that I recorded. If you're a business owner and you're making over $1 million in revenue, you are not going to want to miss this. In this training, I demonstrate the seven most critical elements every business must do in order to go from $1 million to $125 million. Learn in forty minutes what took me years and millions of dollars to figure out, yours completely free.

NINEFIGURETOOLS.COM